DECISION MAKER

An Umpire's Story

DARRELL HAIR

DECISION MAKER

An Umpire's Story

DARRELL HAIR

RANDOM HOUSE
AUSTRALIA

Published by
Random House Australia Pty Ltd
20 Alfred Street, Milsons Point, NSW 2061
http://www.randomhouse.com.au

Sydney New York Toronto
London Auckland Johannesburg
and agencies throughout the world

First published 1998

National Library of Australia
Cataloguing-in-Publication Data

Hair, Darrell.
  Decision Maker: an umpire's story.

  ISBN 0 091 83731 6.

  1. Hair, Darrell. 2. Cricket – Anecdotes. 3. Cricket –
  Australia – Biography. 4. Cricket – Umpiring – Australia –
  Biography. I. Title.

796.42092

Design by Yolande Gray
Typeset by Asset Typesetting Pty Ltd, Sydney
Printed by Griffin Press Pty Ltd

10 9 8 7 6 5 4 3 2 1

CONTENTS

Acknowledgements

Choosing to write this book was the easy part. Choosing who to thank was not so easy. When I sat down to list all of the people who have helped me, not only in cricket but with life in general, the task became daunting. I say sorry to the people I have missed mentioning here but I hope you will understand.

My initial interest in cricket was kindled by big brother, Denis and encouraged by my long suffering mother who recently has not known where in the world I have been (don't worry, mum, the postcards are on the way). Denis provided the taxi to Saturday morning games and anywhere else I needed to go and was instrumental in keeping my interest in cricket on a high. He became an umpire while I was still playing in Orange.

I only became a success at umpiring because of the brotherly traits he passed on to me

To Anne who helped me through the early disappointments and provided me with the inspiration to continue when things got tough—I could not have done it without you.

Being able to swim in the Caribbean and visit the game parks of Africa was, I hope, a fitting reward for putting up with me. Thanks for the support.

To Carl Sharpe from the Orange City Cricket Club who treated me like a father and nurtured some on field talent—the days playing at Molong, Cargo and Cumnock were so special. I thank you a million, Carl. To Bob O'Donnell and Terry Rayner, thanks for ensuring I saw every hotel bar in Orange and anywhere else for that matter.

All of my team mates in Orange, North Sydney and Mosman clubs who played their part in building up my character, if not my ability, during all those late night post match 'celebrations'. At North Sydney Club a particular thanks to team mates Steve Millar and Ross Chapman who showed me the 'bright lights of Sydney' when I was just a lost country boy and to Bevan White who doesn't know it but he became my Sydney father.

At Mosman there was Russell Ewing who helped continue the tradition of late nights and 'just one more port for the road' but was more importantly a great team mate and a terrific friend. Russell together with Greg (Bishan Bedi) Simpson and Jim Tait, (who was actually responsible for me taking up umpiring) formed a fiercesome team of punters which wiled away the winters. Pity about the lack of winners.

Then there are the umpires—Ted Wykes (OAM) and Dick French (OAM) who played such a big part in my early education and steered me in the right direction. Peter

McConnell who got me through my first test and then promptly retired—sorry Peter I didn't know it was such a strain on you. Alan Marshall, Vice President of the NSW Cricket Umpires' Association for his expert training on the laws and on field techniques.

A very special thanks to Ian Thomas and Graham Reed for smoothing the rough edges off my on-field technique. But finally to everybody involved with umpiring in Sydney, New South Wales, Australia and the International Cricket Council (ICC)—thank you for having the faith in me.

In relation to this book I must thank the people at Random House, in particular, Deb Callaghan for her patience which I must have sorely tested at times. To Mark Ray for his valuable notes and assistance and Leo Karis for somehow keeping his sanity.

Introduction

Cricket umpires are widely considered to be conservative, dour, humourless characters who never seem to be enjoying themselves. All around them there is excitement as ferocious struggles unfold involving the best players the world has to offer, yet the umpire still seems somehow detached or removed from the action.

This package is seen on television and at cricket grounds globally as the battle for world supremacy is played out with a competitiveness that could never have been envisaged by the original pioneers of the game. When the first set of laws were written for cricket in 1744 they empowered the umpires to adjudicate in disputes and it was decreed that the umpire's decision 'will be final'. Nothing has changed to alter that fact and it remains so today.

Nevertheless, umpires in the 1990's know the truth—

that many of their decisions are discussed, disputed and questioned in bars after Test matches and at village greens alike. 'I never touched it you know' or 'it must have been missing leg stump' being all too familiar refrains. Umpires are mostly forgotten (or at the least barely tolerated) until there is a flurry of bats, pads, balls and stumps with the famous 'Howzat' appeal quickly following. At that crucial moment all eyes are on the umpire and a split second decision must be made. International and Test Umpires know that making the wrong decision means that the dreaded television replays and cricket commentators will show no mercy in their judgement of the umpire from the safety of their commentary boxes on high. So why do we do it?

In this book I hope to explain some of the reasons why I have found ten years of umpiring in first class cricket to be so completely rewarding. I had boyhood dreams of donning the baggy green cap but there was the simple matter of a considerable lack of ability. To have achieved international status and recognition as an umpire has been the next best thing to playing and has allowed me to visit the places I had only ever dreamed about.

On the following pages I will tell you the truth about the 'throwing affair' which involved more politics and backroom meetings than the Bodyline Series of the 1930s. I also explore the battle for supremacy between McGrath, Warne and the Waugh Brothers as well as revisiting their clashes with Lara, Ambrose, Walsh, Atherton and Tendulkar. I write, too, of the tremendous powers of concentration of Michael Atherton and the warhorse deeds of Angus Fraser. Other chapters in the story of my umpiring career include the drama of the Australia

Day loss in 1994 by the smallest margin in test match history and my views on South Africa formed partly by the dubious privilege of having had a none too complimentary song written about me by a South African radio station. Umpiring with the legendary Dickie Bird at Lords was another highlight that I have the pleasure to relive in this book.

The job of umpiring has never been easy, and with modern technology enabling detailed analysis of every single decision, it will inevitably become much more taxing and difficult in the future. It may seem so simple from the armchair back home but I can assure you this is not the case out there in the middle.

Cricket has given me a thoroughly enjoyable but sometimes rollercoaster ride through life. I hope you enjoy the journey as much as I have.

CHAPTER ONE

BALLS AND
NO BALLS

MCC Laws of Cricket
Law 24.2 Fair Delivery
The Arm

For a delivery to be fair the ball must be bowled not thrown—see note (a) below.
If either umpire is not entirely satisfied with the absolute fairness of a delivery in this respect he shall call and signal 'no ball' instantly upon delivery.

Note (a): Definition of a throw

A ball shall be deemed to have been thrown if, in the opinion of either umpire, the process of straightening the bowling arm, whether it be partial or complete, takes place during that part of the delivery swing which directly precedes the ball leaving the hand. This definition shall not debar a bowler from the use of the wrist in the delivery swing.

Sports mad Melbourne has a tradition on Boxing Day. The cricket fans flock in their thousands to the Melbourne Cricket Ground (MCG) with their hampers of Christmas leftovers. They form a crowd which is as large as any you will see for a Test Match during the Australian summer. The mood is lively—almost celebratory—and 26 December 1995 was no exception as 55 000 fans rolled up despite predictions of a one-sided contest following the Perth Test in which the Sri Lankans had been so soundly beaten.

I must admit to not sleeping much the previous night as I had some very worrying concerns on my mind. I travelled from Sydney on Christmas day and had an early dinner with my colleague, Steve Dunne from New Zealand and the International Cricket Council (ICC) Referee, Graham Dowling. My thoughts were continually returning to the Singer Trophy Tournament held in Sharjah during the previous October. As one of three umpires appointed by the ICC to that Tournament, along with Nigel Plews and Steve Dunne, I had seen off-spinner Muttiah Muralidharan bowl for Sri Lanka.

During the Tournament there was considerable discussion between Nigel, Steve and myself about Muralidharan's bowling action and eventually we resolved to approach the ICC Referee, Raman Subba Row to express our concerns. Raman did not appear to be surprised by our thoughts and subsequently arranged for extensive slow motion video tape to be obtained during the next game.

The idea behind obtaining this footage, which the ICC had agreed to do during August, was to provide the home cricket board of any player considered to have a doubtful bowling action with the tape and the umpire's reports so that

steps could be taken to modify the bowler's action and hopefully avoid the possibility of being 'no-balled' for throwing in
a Test match.

This procedure would, of course, only be successful if the
relevant home cricket board acted swiftly to ensure the player
altered or modified his action to some extent. Sri Lankan
authorities, however, chose to ignore the very clear alarm bells
which had been rung discreetly in their direction. The reasons
they chose not to heed the warnings are only known to those
officials concerned. Their inaction surprises me still especially
given that three of the people who received the warning from
the ICC were the Sri Lankan coach Dav Whatmore, the team
manager Duleep Mendis, and their captain, Arjuna Ranatunga. These people are clearly influential people in Sri
Lankan cricket.

When the Sri Lankan squad arrived in Australia they
were immediately placed under close scrutiny by the media
and some of their bowlers were singled out for their 'funny'
actions. It was certainly no surprise to me that I was not the
only one with doubts about some of the Sri Lankan bowling
actions. Nevertheless the Sri Lankans appeared to be quite
content with their selected team and made no secret of the fact
that Muralidharan would be playing in the Tests

I had viewed my appointment to umpire a World Series
One Day match in Sydney on 8 December between Australia
and Sri Lanka with some misgiving. Still, I was determined to
go into the match with a clear mind. Having not seen
Muralidharan bowl on the tour so far I reasoned that some
modification of his action may have taken place which would
enable me to rule it as being legal. I decided to have a close,

careful inspection of his bowling action from both the bowler's end and at square leg. I came to the conclusion that, if anything, the action was now even more pronounced than it had been in Sharjah.

Critics have always asked why I didn't no ball him that day. With hindsight I should have called him during his eighth and tenth overs—I still have the tape of that game and I feel his action was diabolical. I declined to invoke the very clear laws of the game which prohibit throwing as I still believed that the whole tricky matter could be resolved behind the scenes. Following that One Day match I had a long discussion with Graham Dowling, the ICC Match Referee, but it was made very clear to me that he would not be intervening. He advised that matters such as this must be dealt with on the field according to the laws of the game.

My conclusion after hearing Graham's views was that I would be left alone to do whatever I decided was right on the field if the same situation arose again. This put me in a different situation to what I had previously experienced in my dealings with ICC Referees. In the past they were always up front about not interfering and that included Graham. What he did not say this time was that whatever I did I would have his full support. Sometimes it is the words that are left unsaid that can be the most important.

I realised now that if I was to stand by my firm beliefs and uphold what I knew were the rules of the game, I would have to take action alone on the field. I had just watched someone bowl illegally for ten overs with a mistaken belief that someone else would solve the problem. I did not have long to contemplate my predicament as my invitation to umpire the Boxing Day Test arrived soon after from the Australian Cricket Board (ACB).

Eleven a.m. on match day rolled around far too quickly and I found myself taking the long walk down the ramp and onto the field to start the game. 'The ball must be bowled, not thrown' were the words running through my mind as I took up my position. Mark Taylor had won the toss and decided to bat. Mark would undoubtedly have been very pleased to win the toss but silently I cursed him for his luck on the fall of the coin. That toss only succeeded in pitch-forking me head on into a situation I had been dreading since the One Day match.

Muralidharan came on to bowl from my end mid-way between lunch and tea. The first couple of overs were as I had expected. Initially he bowled with a bent arm which I believe is perfectly legal. As he warmed up and attempted to impart more spin, the arm straightened fractionally, and progressively becoming more definitely 'illegal'. I struggled to find a solution and even considered mentioning my 'problem' to the Sri Lankan captain, Arjuna Ranatunga with a request that he not let Muralidharan bowl again.

This was a Test match however, and I doubted that such a conversation should take place, let alone work. History now records that I called Muralidharan seven times during the next three overs. The balls called were 4 and 6 of his fourth over, 2, 4, 6 of his fifth over and 2 and 6 of his sixth over. In reality I could have called him twenty-seven times or even more. I did not want the matter to become a complete farce as I was certain his captain would simply remove him from the attack. Arjuna left the field, consulted with team management, and returned with the remarkable decision that he would bowl Muralidharan from the other end.

This decision by Ranatunga was extraordinary and inflammatory as he was putting enormous pressure on Steve Dunne. The normal result of a bowler being called for throwing is that his captain would accept the decision and remove him from the attack.

For some reason my mind flashed back to the time Ritchie Benaud removed Ian Meckiff when he was called four times in one over by Col Egar some twenty-five years earlier. Meckiff was taken off by Benaud and never played first class cricket again. I hoped fervently that this would not be the case here.

I must admit I felt stunned and somewhat devastated. I was unsure how Steve would view the situation as we had not discussed the matter prior to the game. I felt to do so would be trying to force my own views on to someone else. Apart from telling Steve after the first couple of calls that I had called him for throwing, I had not considered he would be dragged into the controversy in this way. The concerns which Steve had expressed to me during the Sharjah tournament did not cross my mind at this pressured moment.

When it became clear that Steve was not going to call him I should have continued to make the calls from square leg. This would have left Arjuna with no option but to remove Muralidharan from the attack. However, as the tea break was nearing, I thought, perhaps naively, that I may have one last chance of resolving the matter off the field given the sequence of events which had just unfolded on the field.

During the break I again spoke to ICC Referee, Graham Dowling and basically pleaded with him to request that the Sri Lankan management instruct Arjuna not to bowl him again. The reason for this request was that it was obvious to me that Arjuna was not the man in charge even though he was the appointed captain on the field. It seemed clear that Arjuna took instructions from his administrators which to me indicates a lack of on-field control.

Unfortunately, the referee did not agree with my ideas about how the matter was to be resolved and he reiterated that matters such as this should be settled on the field. It is now history that Muralidharan bowled another twenty or so overs from the members' end without further incident. I did not call him from square leg as I firmly believed the best place to view most suspect actions was from behind the bowler. This later attracted criticism as in the past it has always been considered desirable to make calls on illegal bowling from the square leg or point position.

One journalist even referred to the position behind the bowler's arm as 'The Grassy Knoll'. I actually thought this was quite humorous at the time even though the suggestion being made was that my situation was reminiscent of the alleged area from which the United States President, J.F. Kennedy was assassinated. While imagery of assassinations hardly seems appropriate for cricket, it does indicate the level of furore surrounding the 'Muralidharan affair'

After the tea break I informed the acting captain, Aravinda de Silva, that if Muralidharan bowled again from either end, I would not hesitate to no ball him. This was by no means the ideal way to finalise the matter but I felt the situation was now farcical as Muralidharan had continued to deliver the ball with the same action that I clearly considered to be very much illegal. It was obvious that I was alone in my views with no evident support from the referee or from the Sri Lankan management who appeared determined to isolate and intimidate me. The tea and lunch breaks were a strain for the rest of the game as both teams and the umpires eat in the one dining room. I was determined not to retreat into despondency and continued to visit the dining room for the remainder of the game despite the incredulous looks and sometimes rudeness from the Sri Lankan team and press writers.

The Secretary of the BCCSL Mr Anura Tennakoon publicly stated that I should have slipped them a note prior to the test if I had problems. Mr Tennakoon, I say to you now that my notes were sent to you through the ICC—the appropriate channel for the passing of such information. I am not so sure that 'the note' would have made any difference as Mr Tennakoon told the media in unequivocal terms that they would be the ones to decide whether Muralidharan's action has contravened law 24.2.

The tour management and officials of the Board of Control for Cricket for Sri Lanka (BCCSL) will view the video tape on slow motion and if we feel that his action has not flouted the law then we will consider playing 'Murali' in whatever match in future games, said Tennekoon.

Up until that time I had remained confident that the umpires were the only ones whose views would be taken into account.

The sad thing about the controversy is that there was so much quality cricket played during the Test but not many people remember the general course of the match. The highlights were David Boon regaining form with a hard fought 110, Steve Waugh's usual weighty contribution with 131 not out, Gurusinha fighting hard in the second innings with 143 and the hostile bowling of Glen McGrath who took 7 wickets in the match.

I will never forget a lethal spell McGrath bowled to Tillekeratne who withstood the onslaught with great courage. McGrath struck Tillekeratne several times on the body in a hostile attack, presumably as a result of his failing to walk when he chipped a catch in the One Day match in Sydney. It was probably the quickest bowling I have ever seen but the gutsy left-hander stood firm. Glen came of age as a genuine world class bowler in the match. Mark Taylor completing a hundred catches was another milestone that received little recognition.

The remainder of the game went smoothly for me with all decisions being generally accepted as correct. This was extremely gratifying as it would have been all too easy to dwell on the controversy and let the ball by ball decisions fall apart. I was determined that I would not make a real mess of the game.

I had little care for how the press would report the events but I must admit I was totally stunned by the way a couple of writers went after me. It was as if I was the villain just for trying to do my job. Commonsense went out the window as I found myself under pressure to explain my decisions over and over in public. Some of the adverse reports came from the same reporters who had cast doubts on the legality of Muralidharan's action in the early part of the tour. I can understand their job is to sell newspapers but surely they must have some objectivity and honesty in the articles they write.

In particular two journalists from different newspapers seemed to have exclusive access to the management of the Sri Lankan team. There are battles fought around the world solely in the print media and this appeared to be what was happening now. What many people forgot was the damning evidence which was available in the television footage. The saying 'a picture is worth a thousand words' is certainly applicable in this case—and a moving picture at that.

The most laughable article was an often quoted doctor's report which stated categorically that it was impossible for Muralidharan to fully straighten his arm due to a birth defect. A photo backed up this report with diagrams, set squares, graphs. It was never an issue for me that his arm could not be fully straightened as a partial straightening is all that is necessary to constitute a throw. I have fairly conclusive evidence about Muralidharan's action in the form of a Channel 9 video of him throwing a ball back from the outfield. His arm bends considerably in the wind-up to the throw and ends up by straightening which is what a throw really is.

The media hysteria was manageable but I was terrified when I received death threats delivered to my home through the mail, even placed in my letterbox without stamps. This was frightening stuff as at the time I had an unlisted telephone number and no information about umpires addresses should be available through the State or National Cricket Boards.

I suppose however, if someone really wants to track you down they can through other means.

These threats affected my day-to-day life for a considerable period and I really had to think seriously about whether it was all worth it. Did I really want to continue? It was not much fun leaving home for work each morning wondering if your family will be safe or your house will be intact when you return. The fact that some of these threats contained information only those close to me could have known was also disturbing. The threats were passed on to the Australian Federal Police but I held out little hope of them being traced. In my darkest moments I wondered what had become of cricket.

The whole affair quickly ceased to be a cricket matter and became a political and religious hot potato. The privileged columnists with a pipeline of propaganda direct from the Sri Lankans thought they had found paradise. They had a field day. They even highlighted the fact that Muralidharan was the only Tamil in the team suggesting, incorrectly, a racial base for my decisions. I was unaware of this irrelevant fact until it was reported.

They only seemed interested in reporting how the victimisation was premeditated. There was even a suggestion of some pressure exerted from within the Australian team. I can only reject those accusations. I considered taking legal action for some time. Finally I chose not to proceed with legal action as this would only have created further opportunities for the same journalists, of whom I had such a poor opinion, to continue with their wild theories. I still do not speak to those writers but I do have the courage to look them in the eye.

The conspiracy theory was not helped by an article in the Sydney *Daily Telegraph* on 28 December 1995 in which Allan Border was quoted under the heading:

BORDER CLAIMS CHUCK SET UP

The article went as follows:

Former Test skipper Allan Border yesterday joined the tidal wave of opinion condemning the Muttiah Muralidharan throwing charges as farcical.

Border, who has played more Tests than anyone in history said the Sri Lankan had been set up.

'I know they've been talking about this guy's action since he's come into Test cricket as being a little suspect and it is a very, very different action' Border said on Radio 2UE last night.

'I'm not convinced that he straightens his elbow all the time. I think occasionally he might—which constitutes a throw—but if I were an umpire I wouldn't be prepared to call him. I think it's been a bit of a set up'.

But Border lamented the trap had backfired badly to the detriment of the game worldwide. 'I feel sorry for the umpire because obviously he's been, you know, wound up to do it,' Border said.

Strangely enough Border did not elaborate on how he came to the conclusion it had been a set up. He had no proof and was obviously speculating. In saying that Muralidharan didn't straighten his arm all the time, he is really saying he would not call him if he were an umpire. That is fair enough. If Allan had been an umpire I would not have thought any less of him for holding that opinion. I don't think Muralidharan straightens his arm all the time either—just on some occasions, which is enough for me to make the call. Funny how your support can come from a hostile source. I don't have any problem with other umpires having differing views providing they stick to them.

Border went on to say 'It has left a bit of a sour taste in everyone's mouth that it has come to this where an umpire at the bowler's end, which has never happened before, is calling the bloke'.

My response to that has to be that Border was unaware of the umpires' duties as they work together in a 'team'. The law quite clearly empowers either umpire to make a call. Border was never backward in offering advice to umpires when he was captain so it came as no great surprise that he would have such a firm opinion. He always gave out plenty on the field if he thought you had stuffed up. He was given the tag 'The Third Umpire' from a good number of my colleagues.

Finally, on the conspiracy theory that it was a 'set up', I reject that totally. Apart from my documented discussions with ICC referees, I had never spoken to anyone prior to that match either from within the ACB or the Australian team.

There were many other views and theories. Almost everyone seemed to have one. Richie Richardson, captain of the touring West Indies team weighed in with his view:

> He's just unorthodox. When I look at the slow motion picture I don't really think he chucks. He comes over with a lightly bent arm and when he releases the ball his wrist straightens. But if you look really carefully, the arm remains bent.

A different view again. I find it difficult to believe Richardson was watching the same video tapes as I was.

Others to have their say were two former Australian off-spinners, Bruce Yardley and Ashley Mallett. Yardley said:

> *We should be celebrating his action not trying to run him out of the game. There is no way that Muttiah has to change his action. If he straightened his arm like they say he does the ball would go 50 metres over the wicket keeper's head.*

Some strange analysis here. Notice that Yardley has introduced the anonymous 'they' which can mean almost anybody you want it to mean. Why the ball would sail over the keeper's head is a mystery to me. Then again, Yardley did in fact coach Sri Lanka some seven years ago with Muralidharan under his control.

Ashley Mallett had a different view:

> *I think he looks very suspect. He definitely straightened his arm,*

This was all Mallett would say. Two opposing views but who is right?

Former players and commentators came out of the woodwork to have their say and, to my surprise, out of the ashes came a few who publicly supported me. People such as Ken Stackpole who is always willing to bag poor umpiring had this to say under the following *Herald-Sun* headline on 8 January:

HAIR NOT OUT OF PLACE

Countries which tip the bucket on umpires should be disciplined by cricket's ruling body, the International Cricket Council (ICC). Following the vicious and scathing attacks on Australian umpire Darrell Hair, the ICC should take a tough stand against countries who breach the code of conduct and protect its members on the international panel of umpires.

The Hobart *Mercury* carried this report on 9 January:

Ken Rutherford, former New Zealand captain believes Muttiah Muralidharan is a blatant chucker whose action should never be tolerated in international cricket. Rutherford has been the first current first class cricketer to openly criticise Muralidharan since the off-spinner was called for chucking. Rutherford, who quit New Zealand several months ago to play for Transvaal in South Africa, became so frustrated with Muralidharan's action his patience snapped in a one day international in South Africa two years ago. After dead batting a Muralidharan delivery to his feet, he picked up the ball and bowled it back to Muralidharan with an obvious bent arm. He was later fined 75 per cent of his match fee by referee Peter Burke for bringing the game into disrepute.

'I don't think he should have been allowed to

bowl in Test cricket because I don't think his action is legitimate,' Rutherford said.

'At earlier stages of his career he should have been given the chance to change it. It is pretty obvious to most people watching television with the benefit of slow motion replays and different angles on his action there is a distinct bent elbow there that straightens as the ball is bowled. The whole New Zealand team considered he chucked it when we played Sri Lanka in New Zealand last year.' Rutherford's strong feelings are laced with deep sympathy.

'I feel a lot of sympathy for him because I don't think anyone would say he is doing it intentionally. He just picked up an action when he was a little kid in backyard games. It's a bit unfortunate—during the early day of his career when he could have corrected it, no-one was around to coach him and correct him.'

Yes, there was someone, Ken. Where were you when you were needed Mr Yardley?

Rutherford, like myself, does not accept the argument that Muralidharan, because he is a spinner, does not profit from an illegal action as much as a paceman would. If by using an illegal action, a spinner gains more assistance with turn and bounce than he would with a normal offie, it is still gaining an advantage. To me it should not matter whether some one is bowling at 90 or 50 miles an hour—if it is against the laws then it should not be allowed.

I found many supportive comments heartening and they gave me the incentive and drive to continue umpiring the game I love so much.

At the conclusion of the Test match, the Sri Lankan management requested a meeting with me to ascertain which deliveries I had been concerned about. They reasoned that if they had this information then they could remedy the situation. I was taken aback by their request as all they had to do was study the deliveries I had called. Even so, as I have always been a 'one ball at a time' umpire I could not see how such a meeting would achieve anything. While I would have been willing to discuss the matter with them I am sure I would not have been able to offer much assistance. In any event the ACB refused the request by saying that it would set a precedent to allow questioning of umpires' decisions during or after every game.

With the Test match completed, the One Day Series was still to be finalised. I was to figure prominently in these matches as the ACB had already made the appointments. Sri Lanka attempted to have me removed from future games but the ACB stood firm and insisted I would fulfil my appointments. Richard Watson, Operations Manager for the ACB, was quoted in a newspaper printed outside Australia:

> *Any request to have Hair replaced will be rejected. They can have whatever they want on their wish list, but playing conditions state that neither team will have the right to object to an umpire's appointment.*

This report was not included in any Australian newspapers which was a shame for me but the ACB would have had their reasons for keeping it quiet in this country. I was grateful for this show of support and the backing of the ICC on the whole incident. ICC issued a statement which pinpointed the reports which had been made and confirmed that referees and umpires had been indicating concerns about Muralidharan's action for at least eighteen months prior to the Boxing Day Test. The ICC statement read as follows:

> *The ICC has been aware of for some time of speculation as to the legitimacy of this player's bowling action and has taken the following steps.*
>
> *In 1993, the ICC Referee Peter Burge spoke privately with several of the (previous) Administration of the Sri Lankan Board to relay his doubts arising from having watched the player bowl in the home series against India.*
>
> *In March 1995, when Sri Lanka toured New Zealand, ICC Referee Barry Jarman was so concerned that he arranged for a slow motion*

video tape of the bowler's action to be taken. This tape was forwarded through ICC to BCCSL.

These steps were taken in the player's interest.

When Sri Lanka participated in the Sharjah One Day Series in early October, the three umpires, Darrell Hair, Nigel Plews and Steve Dunne advised the ICC Referee Raman Subba Row of their concern and further footage was obtained which has been passed on to the BCCSL. Subba Row spoke to the Sri Lankan manager and coach at the end of the series.

ICC has been informed by the BCCSL that the video footage has been reviewed and understand that the player has been informed, though we do not know whether the player has seen the video or been advised of a number of umpire's concerns about his action.

These steps have been taken in the player's interest to try and avoid him being called for an illegal delivery in International Cricket.

Nonetheless, it is every umpire's duty to apply the laws of cricket fully and impartially and we stand in full support of these umpire's who execute this responsibility to the best of their ability. The relevant law is clear and the game of cricket cannot accept any breach of this law.

To me this statement says it all but there were many who wanted to stick their head in the sand and deny or forget that this was not recent news yet rather it was a controversy which had been brewing for quite some time.

The ACB were also in a difficult position. There was something that I had not considered which was the involvement of Australia in the upcoming World Cup. Australia was to play their first qualifying match in Colombo.

Muralidharan subsequently played in Hobart and was not called by umpires Terry Prue and Steve Davis. I have been asked many times how I felt after that match. I have no feelings either way, I only wanted to have the full story to be told in one place. The Hobart match certainly disproves the conspiracy theory that Australian umpires where out to crucify him. Each umpire may have a differing view and we sometimes see or interpret things in a different way to each other. Terry Prue, Steve Davis and Steve Dunne are proof of that.

Ross Emerson and Tony McQuillan also saw things in another light when a few days later they decided that what they were seeing was illegal. I think the Australian umpires have shown they will make their own decisions and not let others dictate to them. That is our right under the clear laws of the game.

Following the World Series match in Perth on 12 January I found the Sri Lankans had lodged an official complaint about my 'behaviour'. Prior to the match, the referee had expressed concern about the use of substitute fieldsmen and told us to crack down on the practice of bowlers leaving the field straight after they had completed a few overs. This has always been a problem area for umpires as players are quite entitled to leave the field for a legitimate injury or illness. We are not qualified in medicine and a request to leave the field to have a knee treated, a finger taped or just the normal toilet break is always allowed. The situation is open to abuse, of course. Following Graham Dowling's directive to us in Perth both Peter Parker and myself were continually asking the captain Aravinda de Silva why players were leaving the field and when they were expected back. Aravinda obviously took exception to this and became agitated at the questions.

The matter is probably best summed up by two newspaper reports, the first by by Michael Koslowski of the *Sydney Morning Herald* (13 January 1998) which read:

> *Sri Lankan outrage with umpire Darrell Hair has reached boiling point, with the tourists calling for him to be banned from officiating in any more of their matches on tour. They also want Hair reprimanded over what they claim to be the offensive way in which he spoke to acting Captain Aravinda de Silva in a heated exchange between the pair. The Sri Lankan's simmering anger reached a climax during Friday's loss to Australia. The forty-three-year-old umpire reprimanded de Silva for the regular flow of Sri Lankan players leaving the field for breaks*

The second report from Robert 'Crash' Craddock of the Sydney *Daily Telegraph* (13 January 1998) adds some further facts and balance:

> *Sri Lanka's ill-fated tour of Australia was rocked by another controversy yesterday when Vice Captain Aravinda de Silva was reported for vandalising a dressing-room. The West Australian Cricket Association confirmed last night the Sri Lankans would be billed for damage created by a furious de Silva after he was dismissed for a duck on Friday night.*
>
> *The rampage started in the players' dressing room where plates and glasses were shattered before de Silva went upstairs to the viewing room and belted a glass window with his bat. The panel was dinted and chipped and when match officials were alerted to the damage they referred the matter to the WACA.*
>
> *De Silva, at loggerheads with umpire Darrell Hair throughout the Australian innings was inconsolable after being given out LBW by Hair off Stuart Law's gentle medium pace in a borderline decision.*
>
> *De Silva glared back at Hair several times as he left the field. The Sri Lankans yesterday confirmed their willingness to press ahead with a complaint to the ACB about Hair scheduled to stand in the tourist's final World Series Cricket (WSC) match at the MCG. They wanted Hair*

25

removed from tomorrow's game and charged with misconduct. They claim he has become arrogant and dismissive towards them in on field matters.

These two reports when put together give a pretty clear picture of what had occurred. Firstly, I had been given an instruction by the referee to stamp out an unsportsman-like practice which is of course the domain of umpires anyway. I might have known it would not be easy to start hassling captains half way through a tour about what was to them a minor matter. Secondly, and more importantly, I think the whole request to have me removed was only brought up to deflect publicity away from de Silva's rampage. Players quite often damage dressing rooms in their frustration and the actions have been called childish, however I can sympathise with them when they fail to perform at that very elite level. It is a game played for high stakes and the honour of doing well for your country. Failure is pretty hard to take for both players and umpires.

I make no apologies for giving the LBW decision and for all I know, de Silva may have been just annoyed about getting out to the gentle medium pace of Stuart Law.

During this game however, Peter Parker and myself made out official reports to ICC regarding two other Sri Lankan bowlers, Dharmasena and Kalpage. We considered their bowling actions to be also very doubtful, in particular Dharmasena. Our report stated that urgent attention should be paid to our views as if either player were to bowl with the same action again we would have no hesitation in invoking Law 24 by calling them for throwing. We suggested that the matter be dealt with by the ICC representative, Graham

Dowling which was probably a mistake as he had not shown much authority during the season. He was, I believe still suffering from the way he botched the ball tampering incident in Perth during the Test, however he did take possession of the reports and so we held out some hope of a resolution.

Steve Randell and myself were in Melbourne the following Tuesday and we were summoned from the breakfast table at our hotel for an urgent meeting with Graham Halbish, the CEO of the Australian Cricket Board. On our arrival in his office, Graham Dowling joined us and our report from Perth was discussed. It was obvious Halbish and Dowling did not want us to take any action. Halbish said that while it was up to the umpires to apply the laws of the game and the ACB would always support umpires who did so, we could find ourselves 'between a rock and a hard place'. I then realised we may well be left out to dry with no prospect of support and that hurt me immensely.

This was so disappointing as it now appeared that world cricket considered the issue as being too hard (or hot) to handle. It was also obviously preferable for the umpires controlling games to ignore the throwing law at least until the World Cup had been completed. Had I known then that Australia would boycott the games scheduled in Sri Lanka I would have done things differently and called any bowler whose action did not comply with the law.

As it transpired no other action would be taken for the rest of the tour. I know for a fact that I was fed up and felt there had been more than enough controversy. The game could certainly do without any further bad publicity. I understand the issue of a harmonious World Cup would have been foremost in the minds of administrators but it did not make the matter any more palatable or acceptable to me. I firmly believe the behind the scenes dealings did much more damage to the game and that the niggling tactics of the Sri Lankans who chose to fight a political battle via the press was a disgrace. The fact that the ICC representative in Australia at the time allowed certain things to go unchecked only fuelled the fire. At one stage I faxed a copy of statements made by Dav Whatmore, Arjuna Ranatunga and Muralidharan which were a clear breach of the ICC Code of Conduct but nothing was done. Section 2 of the code refers to players and team officials and states in part that 'Players and team Officials shall not engage in conduct unbecoming which could bring the game into disrepute'.

Prior to the Finals of the World Series cup, the ACB and the Management of the Sri Lankan team arranged a meeting which I had been invited to attend. This followed a meeting the previous day between the Sri Lankans and ACB Chief Executive Graham Halbish. I can only guess about what was discussed at that meeting, but I'm sure my name came up somewhere.

The meeting to which I was invited was held at the MCG shortly before the last World Series qualifying match and captains, managers and coaches were able to air their grievances. The various aspects of the summer were discussed, in particular my actions which had been wrongly interpreted as 'harrassment'. The air was cleared and Sri Lanka went on to win the game.

The other thing mentioned was the deterioration in the friendliness and sportsmanship between the two teams. I presume I was invited because I was deemed to have contributed to this ill feeling. I felt insulted by my inclusion in the meeting and felt it was a slight on my position as an international umpire. I attended however, and it was agreed that both teams would bury the hatchet and mix socially after each of the finals. I cannot help feeling though that a few people in the room from both sides of the fence really wanted the hatchet buried all right—fairly and squarely between my eyes.

The first final in Melbourne went off smoothly but during the second final in Sydney two nights later, umpires Randell and Parker refused to allow a runner for Arjuna Ranatunga.

Arjuna had certainly been puffing after running a few quick singles and it is a fine line between knowing whether a request for a substitute runner is genuine or not. In this case only Ranatunga will really know but it sparked some more controversy and this time I was only sitting in the third umpire's box! I was named on banners around the ground proclaiming me as 'Man of the Match' and even 'Man of the Series'.

At the conclusion of the game and at the presentation to Australia for winning the series, Arjuna and his team refused to shake hands with Mark Taylor and the rest of the

Australians. Sore losers or just bad sportsmanship—again only Arjuna will know.

What caused me the most anguish during this whole unfortunate period were the activities of Dav Whatmore, the Sri Lankan coach, throughout the summer. He continually denied that he had been told of my concerns in Sharjah when, in fact, in the presence of Duleep Mendis, Arjuna Ranatunga and Whatmore, referee Raman Subba Row informed them as a group, in my presence, about the report.

Whatmore made a meal of the game in Brisbane when Ross Emerson called Muralidharan by trying to video tape the action from the location of deep mid wicket on the boundary. Red faces all round when the batteries on his camera packed up and he failed to get a shot of the action. This little sideshow was also reported to ICC as I considered it a blatant breach of the code of conduct but again no action was taken.

It also begs the question, Why would you try to video tape someone's action from such a strange location? I suppose all he was trying to prove was that if the umpires stood on the deep mid-wicket boundary they would find no problem with his action. An unsatisfactory solution I think.

Whatmore also approached me on the night of the One Day Final at the SCG wanting to know if we could 'get together' to thrash out the problem. The reply I gave him was to the effect that I would only talk to him if and when he was able to supply the media with the whole truth on the matter. I declined his invitation which was probably a good decision.

The initial hysteria would have been more appropriate had I had issued a death sentence by calling Muralidharan. I had done no such thing of course as I do not believe that every delivery was a blatant throw. The only player who would have to give the game away would be the player who throws every single delivery. The fact that Muralidharan, in my opinion, did not do this is a clear indication that he would in all probability continue playing and he has done so. Headlines of an execution were very much out of place.

There is a school of thought however that it is easy to bowl legally when you know you are being filmed but that you may do something completely different when the trial is over. Sort of like driving within the speed limit when a police car is following you. When the University of Western Australia conducted tests in 1996, it came to a conclusion that Muralidharan's arm did not straighten but did add that they could not be certain that his bowling action would not change or deteriorate under the stress of match conditions.

I have not seen Muralidharan bowl since the Melbourne Test three years ago but he has gone on to take over 200 wickets and recently in England took 16 wickets to spin Sri Lanka to a 10 wicket victory at The Oval. Naturally this raised some eyebrows, including those of the England coach David Lloyd who publicly stated that the ICC should look seriously at his bowling action. 'It's the action as well, we have a leg spinner with an orthodox action, they have an off spinner with an unorthodox action. If that's the way to go and if it's OK, then let's find somebody like it', said Lloyd. This is a statement which could be construed as sour grapes, coming hot on the heels of losing a Test match.

The debate over throwing has ebbed and flowed over the years and it appears everyone has and will always be entitled to their own point of view.

In the wake of this incident the ICC changed the wording of Law 24 to provide for the umpire to issue the caution, final warning and removal from the attack. In other words, if three illegal deliveries are called it will now see the bowler out of the attack. This brought throwing into line with other types of illegal bowling such as fast short pitched or fast high full tosses. Bowlers can also be removed from the attack for damaging the pitch. I do not feel proud that I have been responsible for a law of the game being altered but if it helps other umpires to apply the throwing law, then it has been worthwhile. I would never want the same stress, conjecture and controversy to surround the decisions of any umpire in the future.

The views of such respected people as John Benaud and Sir Donald Bradman to me are a fitting way to close the debate. Sir Donald Bradman said in 1960 at a meeting of the International Cricket Conference, later to be renamed International Cricket Council:

> It (throwing) is the most complex question I have known in cricket, because it is not a matter of fact, but of opinion and interpretation. It is so involved that two men of equal goodwill and sincerity could take opposite views.

The meeting minutes also noted:

> It is hoped that all those who may be concerned with the future of cricket will do all in their power to assist those whose admittedly difficult task it is to adjudicate on this problem.

It's hard to believe that Sir Donald made that statement thirty-five years prior to my self and Steve Dunne having opposing views of the same action. Benaud, himself a cricketer of high standard added some sanity to the debate when he said that the best place to view a suspect bowler was from behind the bowler's arm or in front, the view that the batsman gets. As I think standing in front of the batsman would disturb his concentration, I am convinced I made the right choice by utilising 'the grassy knoll' where I would normally stand.

CHAPTER TWO

MEMORIES OF
SOUTH AFRICA

If ever the term 'Bad Hair Day' was to apply to me, it was during the Third Test between Australia and South Africa in Adelaide in 1994. The first Test in Melbourne was marred by rain and only about two days play was possible. The match naturally finished in a draw but I was honoured to umpire it as it marked the return of South Africa to the Test match grounds of Australia.

The South Africans went into the third game on a high after their thrilling 6 run win in Sydney and had every right to he confident of future success. The Aussies had again shown an inability to chase a small target and the wind had been taken from their sails. South Africa were confident of success and they did not mind letting everyone know. Players such as Brian Macmillan, Alan Donald and Hansie Cronje were world class and they were determined to prove their worth.

The fact that this Test was to turn out to be my worst

performance ever annoyed me then and it still does now. Some critics may say I always have shockers but certainly not like this game—it turned into a real nightmare. A couple of decisions went against South Africa and tempers reached boiling point. Umpires' decisions will always be a 'way out' for teams not performing but two of mine were, to put it bluntly, abysmal. The LBW decisions on Hudson and Richardson were, if I could have them over again, the two I wish I hadn't made. The benefit should definitely have gone to the batsmen on those occasions.

Hudson had played well forward to Steven Waugh but was hit directly in line. A lack of complete concentration and focus in that exact moment saw me give him out. Richardson's decision was, quite simply, wrong. Again my concentration went haywire as the ball would not have hit a second set of stumps. The Australian Cricket Board supply umpires with video tape of every game we umpire and we are expected to review and assess our own performances. These personal assessments are then compared with the captains' reports. This process forms a large part of our own development and enables you to analyse your game and locate your weaknesses. After reviewing this particular game on video, I was happy with all of my decisions other than the two I have just noted. Peter Kirsten would not agree.

Peter and I exchanged words after the Hudson dismissal which resulted in a code of conduct charge being brought against him. Peter said 'Why do you give us out and not the Aussies'. Peter may have been just thinking out aloud but the inference from him was that I was being less than fair. He was subsequently given a fine of 25 per cent of his match fee by referee Jackie Hendricks. Umpires may get things wrong due to many factors but I detest being called a cheat. It really goes against the grain because I take my umpiring very seriously and I am not a cheat.

Sometimes a bat sounds like pad and vice versa. You find yourself with your finger pointing skywards when it should be firmly kept in your pocket. I think Kirsten got off lightly. His defence that it was at the end of a long hard tour was not a satisfactory excuse given that he only joined the team as a late replacement in December! Of course, tempers fray out there at this level of the game, but accusations of cheating are another thing altogether.

The episode was repeated in the second innings and after round two of Hair versus Kirsten I gave him out LBW in a perfectly fair call. He left the field at an agonising pace after giving me a mouthful and showing everyone his bat to indicate he had hit the ball. He did in fact hit the ball but *after* the ball had made impact on the pads. Kirsten also gave a well known 'two finger salute' to members of the crowd who suggested he might actually choose to leave the ground as the next batsman was ready to take strike.

The video replays confirmed this to be the case and even though there were two distinct noises, I was happy that even with the naked eye the ball had hit the pad first. Many judges consider that the very fact that there are two noises should leave enough doubt for an umpire to give the benefit to the batsman. Test cricketers, however, feel quite differently and get most annoyed when a clear pad/bat impact is not given. Most of them think umpires take 'the easy way out' with these decisions not to give the batsman out and they quickly lose respect for you as an umpire.

Kirsten's name found it's way onto another report form and a hearing was convened by Jackie Hendricks at the conclusion of the game. This time 40 per cent of his match fee disappeared into ICC coffers which was a punishment I had difficulty coming to terms with. Under normal circumstances a second report for dissent in the same match should result in a suspension. Peter got off lightly in my opinion by only copping another fine which was apparently paid by a radio station in Durban.

Fines do not work unless it is a substantial amount such as the $4 000 levies dished out to Shane Warne and Merv Hughes during the subsequent tour by the Aussies to South Africa. Even then, who is to know whether the player actually pays it himself or a benefactor coughs up on the player's behalf? A percentage of a match fee can in fact be a pittance as some countries pay their Test players very little. Overall, I don't think the fines system works at all—maybe a suspension or two would have achieved the desired effect.

I know the United Cricket Board of South Africa were none too pleased with someone else paying Kirsten's fine. A well known official let it be known that if you do the crime, you do the time.

If I had the game over again I would have done some things differently but who wouldn't? Unfortunately, the South African team lost any respect they had for me over incidents during this game, and basing their view on the way the close ones went against them, who could blame them?

What was even more annoying for me personally was that I had just been nominated by the ACB as one of two umpires on the newly formed ICC Independent Panel. An invitation had been issued to officiate in two Tests in the Caribbean for the series against England so the South African team, and the world for that matter, must have thought umpiring in Australia was very, very poor. On the Adelaide performance I was not up to International standard and this fact hurt me immensely.

Umpires having to put up with crank callers is a constant issue and I copped more than my share after this game. I stayed on in Adelaide for a couple of days to wind down and some friends were looking after my home back in Sydney. They were stunned and frightened when a few nasty and abusive calls came through which was something they should not have had to cope with. That was the start of a silent number routine which I maintain to this day.

In the weeks following the Test I was back in Sydney umpiring club cricket which is the type of thing that really brings you down to earth. The opportunity to be back umpiring grass roots cricket never seemed so attractive. No televison replays and no crowds. Cricketers just enjoying their Saturday afternoon game.

I was still annoyed with myself for putting in such a substandard performance when I attended the launch of Mike Whitney's autobiography *Quick Whit*. Some distinguished players such as Greg Matthews, Geoff Lawson and 'Whit' himself offered encouragement and said that whilst everyone can put in an absolute shocker, the best (umpires and players) will always bounce back. In particular Matthews said, 'So you had a bad day, players have them all the time. What's the big deal?' I appreciated the support and decided to just get on with the job and forget about the past.

Journalist Mark Ray called in on me at the North Sydney No. 2 ground where I was umpiring a third grade clash between North Sydney and Waverley clubs. Some people may say that the standard was just about right for me! It was a time for reflection for me. I had played for the North Sydney club and one of the more enjoyable aspects of being away from Sydney so much is that we are frequently placed in a lower grade match when you return because it is often in the middle of a two day club round.

Mark asked me how I felt about having a quiet day of anonymity at a pleasant suburban club ground far from controversy. I responded that the players here have got just as much right to have a good game of cricket as Test players. That makes it just as important for them to have umpires and if I can play my part here I will be more than happy. This is where I played. I still know a lot of the players so I can't really afford to get one wrong, can I?

I had good intentions for the day but I think I may have 'fired' the Waverley captain LBW which goes to prove that the human error element will always be with us. The measure of a player's character is his ability to come back from a sub-standard performance and prove the critics wrong. I had no option but to do the same and prove to everyone that I was an umpire worthy of doing tests. I knew full well that I was a capable umpire. It was up to me to prove myself again as I knew I had something to offer cricket. I parallel this with a player who desperately wants to perform and win back the confidence of his coach or captain and prove himself worthy.

My confidence and self esteem were low but no-one could do it for me. The West Indies tour came and went without much drama as did a full domestic season in Australia. But I knew that to prove to myself that I was worthy, I had to shake off any thoughts of a recurrence of poor form when I would have to umpire South Africa again.

The opportunity came in New Zealand in 1995. I suppose being away from home and being the 'neutral' umpire, a term I hate, made it easier. The neutral term should be removed from the cricket vocabulary for all time as it has connotations of being the saviour of all cricketers who feel they have been persecuted at some stage. The sticking point with me is that when umpires travel overseas as an ICC panel member, we are quite often standing with another panel member and we are both umpires of equal standing. Even if I were to stand with a non panel member, it surely is an insult for him to be referred as the 'local' umpire, but it still happens. Both umpires do the job as a team and the reason we are appointed according to Law 3.8 is to 'control the game with absolute impartiality as required by the laws.' If any umpire has a problem with that requirement then he should not be in the game. Unfortunately the term 'neutral' is one giant stigma which has not yet disappeared from the game.

The Test at Eden Park came and went without a hitch but it was not until an appointment came to umpire in Johannesburg later that year that I started to feel nervous. The South African public had not in any way forgotten my name and various comments from around the 'bull ring' of the Wanderers Ground made for interesting listening. The 'bull ring' is aptly named and is a hometown advantage used by the South Africans to intimidate their opposition. The ground has that Colosseum flavour and you cannot help feeling that you may be the next sacrifice.

After the Adelaide Test, I had the 'honour' of having a song written about me which I really did enjoy and thought was quite funny. The song was the brainchild of the same radio station in Durban that polled their listeners and took up a collection to pay for Peter Kirsten's fines. The chorus went as follows:

> *Darrell, Darrell what are you doin' out there?*
> *Every time our guys go out to bat, you stick your*
> *finger in the air,*
> *Darrell, Darrell, we'll remember Darrell Hair,*
> *But if you come to South Africa, put your finger*
> *elsewhere.*

The chorus is about all that can be reprinted as the rest degenerates rapidly, though I thought it was quite witty at the time. I sincerely hope the money collected from sales and royalties was donated to charity. If not, then I want my share!

The crowd at the Wanderers Ground found time to repeat the chorus at the slightest opportunity, mainly when I had given a batsman not out which I genuinely took in good humour.

As the game approached I felt like I was under a not inconsiderable amount of pressure and it convinced me that it would in one way or another decide my international future. Had I given a decision with even the slightest hint of doubt, the press, television and the public would have had a field day. One thing I must mention that put my mind somewhat at ease were a couple of telephone calls I received shortly after arrival. One was from Dr Ali Bacher and the other from South African captain, Hansie Cronje. They both welcomed me to their country, gave me their numbers and told me to call should I require any help. Cynics may see this as an attempt to stay on the 'right side' but I know both these men were sincere with their wishes and intent. It did make me feel more confident about the task ahead. It is gestures like these that restore your faith in the cricket community and remind you of what is so appealing about the game even now in the super competitive game it has become.

The match began with South Africa batting and a poor game from me was one thing I decided was totally out of the question. I would have been shown up as a completely incompetent umpire and not just one who was, like most mere

45

mortals, capable of human error. Every ball was clear and concise in my mind and each decision was given after careful consideration of the facts available to me. This was the game when Michael Atherton scored 185 not out and batted for ten hours and forty-five minutes in the final innings to save the game for England. If he could concentrate, then why not me too?.

I thought a lot about what would be going through Atherton's mind at the time. Michael must have amazing powers of concentration and nothing was going to give him cause to let the team down. Atherton took time to draw about him that cloak of utter assurance which he wears during such long innings. Iron will, watertight technique and flawless concentration—if he could summon the strength of mind, why not me? I had only myself to let down and that match taught me a lot about my own powers of concentration. I learned it from Michael. If you want something badly enough it will come but only after the right amount of effort is put in.

South Africa really expected to win but to the annoyance of their fans I did have a good match so they could not blame the umpires. My focus remained steady and solid and it was then that I knew that I had plenty more to offer as an umpire. It's amazing what being shit-scared of doing well on the international stage can do for your powers of concentration.

I even made the papers via the Johannesburg *Saturday Star* on 2 December 1995 when Jack Bannister wrote the following piece under the heading:

HAIR-RAISING DAY FOR DARRELL,
BUT HE DID HIS JOB WELL

Few umpires on the twenty strong ICC International panel have faced greater pressure abroad than Darrell Hair when he walked out at the Wanderers Ground two days ago.

The tall Australian knew that his every move would be monitored by players and spectators alike following several controversial incidents in the Adelaide Test in January, 1994. Peter Kirsten was fined 65 per cent of his match fee by referee Jackie Hendricks for dissent expressed at several LBW decisions, including Kirsten's own in the second innings.

Against England, it was Hair's non use of the third umpire and television assistance in a tight run out which upset England. Mark Taylor was shown to be run out, albeit narrowly, but Hair gave him not out.

Which is why, unusually, both sides in this current Test match raised their eyebrows when his appointment was announced. The ICC appoint umpires and do not consult with the various countries when they decide who will officiate abroad.

The official line is that if a country nominates an umpire as one of its two representatives, his acceptability all around the world must be taken for granted. As David Richards, Chief Executive of

ICC said—once you start asking for this umpire or that, and a country has a right of refusal, the system would fall apart.

Which is why Hair was appointed for the Wanderers Test. He was appointed to the ICC Panel in 1994 after only seven Tests at home. He got through the first day with no problems and no fuss and was within one over of the completion of quite a relaxed second day at the office. What was to happen in the next five balls showed that if an umpire allows his concentration to waiver for a split second, he is gone.

Off the fourth ball of that dramatic final over bowed by Dominic Cork, Brian McMillan played forward and the ball deviated off something to wicket keeper Jack Russell. Cork war-danced his way down the full length of the pitch past the batsman and looked incredulously at Hair when the not out decision was given.

But Hair was right and Cork wrong. What the television slow-motion replay showed was that McMillan, playing forward hid the bat just behind the front pad and the ball had deflected off the pad and not the bat. It would have been easy for Hair to have been seduced into an error by the deflection but he got it right.

He could have been forgiven for running the incident over again in his mind as the irate Cork raced in for the next delivery, having not exactly sprinted back to his mark after the previous ball.

Another ball which moved from outside off-stump, but this time a more tentative stride across from McMillan who collected the ball on the back pad bringing another impassioned appeal from Cork to whom Hair gave the LBW decision.

This ended a good day for him and Karl Leibenberg and for my money they deserve praise and understanding for having the most thankless job in cricket.

Reading this article later I recalled how I felt so alert during the game. It was a feeling you would like to be able to bottle and use at a later time but sadly that is not possible. It was nice, however, to get some good positive press for a change though.

Eighteen months earlier in Adelaide I had done seven Tests and I felt that I had not been prepared for handling the really high pressure situations. I was not so much concerned about making mistakes, but being able to get over it quickly and be ready for the next appeal. It equates to a fieldsman dropping a catch or a bowler being hit for two fours in a row.

In Johannesburg, I had excellent support from my partners Karl Leibenberg, Rudi Koertzen and Barry Lamson who made up the team of television and stand-by umpires. Such teams were not in operation prior to 1994 and it is one of the reasons umpiring has come a long way There is more of a team nature about it now when you include the assistance of the referee as well. I liken the 'team' now to the support Atherton had during his innings from Robin Smith and Jack Russell. Without it, survival is just not possible.

Rudi Koertzen has since made his way onto the ICC panel and has been umpiring with distinction. We have become firm friends and we share similar views. We both understand the high standards of performance which are required for umpiring cricket today. The television exposure, travel and umpiring on new and unfamiliar grounds are just some of the extra demands placed on umpires today.

One of the reasons for things getting out of hand and players berating umpires over decisions on the field is player management off the field. A good coach will realise a talented player is of no use to him if his energy is taken up by continually sniping at umpires. Players too quickly forget that they make mistakes as well. A good management team of captain, coach and possibly even tour manager can quite often defuse a potentially explosive situation before it gains too much momentum.

The personnel in the South African team have changed with Hansie Cronje and Bob Woolmer taking over from Kepler Wessels and Mike Proctor. I know Cronje was captain in Adelaide but it was also his first stint at the captaincy, replacing Wessels who was injured. From my few dealings

'The ball is on its way — and so am I.' Muralidharan bowling in the Australia v Sri Lanka 2nd Test, MCG 1995. Darrell Hair looks on. (*Australian Picture Library*)

Muralidharan's follow-through. (*Australian Picture Library*)

That call. Darrell Hair makes a considered decision. (*Australian Picture Library*)

The Aftermath. Darrell Hair is outnumbered during the no ball incident in Melbourne. Arjuna Ranatunga (Captain) had reinforcements at the ready.

Darrell Hair finally no balls Muralidharan during the 2nd Test, Australia v Sri Lanka. (*Australian Picture Library*)

Discussing the quality of cricket balls with Allan Border. 'Aren't these supposed to be round?'

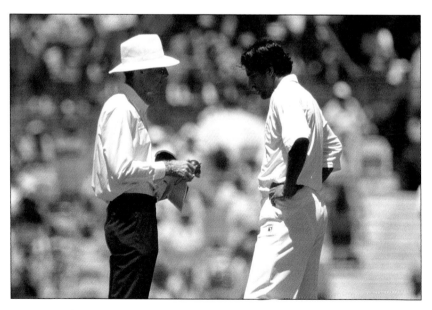

Steve Randell having a similar discussion with Wasim Akram, one of the most dangerous men on the cricket field. Steve is the most laid back.

With Steve Dunne at the MCG on Boxing Day.

Leaving the ground after the Boxing Day match. 'Excuse me, Darrell, would you mind checking out of our hotel now.'

Discussion with Ricky Ponting. 'Who do you think will win the Cup?'

with Wessels, I found him to be a complex character with a brooding nature. He gave me the impression that if you had something to say to him he might just listen, or then again he might not. He was just about impossible to communicate with.

One of the categories umpires are marked on is communication and I cannot for the life of me understand how a captain can give you some sort of mark when he has only spoken to you once or twice in the course of a series. Is this supposed to be one way traffic? Wessels only had something to say when he felt he had copped a rough decision, not if his team mates were on the receiving end—only him!

The only time Wessells spoke to me was to give me a bagging when I gave him out LBW in one of the earlier one day matches. All left-handers believe they are never out anyway even though the same set of circumstances applies to all LBW decisions. I had given him out to a Paul Reiffel in-swinger after he had indeed played forward.

When the ball hit him he was in considerable trouble as the only thing which could have saved him was an inside edge. This wasn't the case and up went my finger. He walked past muttering, 'How can you possibly give that out?' Then he proceeded to give me a pasting in the umpire's report.

Well, Kepler, all I can say is you must have missed the replay, because it was dead straight. I highlight this because he had inherited the Australian way of whingeing about decisions, but most of all he had learnt a lot in his time playing for Australia. This resulted in two teams with identical attitudes. Both always say it is out when you are bowling, but never when you are batting.

Wessels had given Australian umpires a fair serve in his book stating that in his view the Australians always seemed to get a wicket when they needed one. He conveniently overlooked the decisions which may have gone his way during the series and I can think of quite a few that did, but have no intention of listing them here. My overall impression of Wessels was of a man who lacked grace and fairness and his miserable demeanour indicated he seemed to have a very large chip on his shoulder which was never going to be removed.

Things have changed considerably since Hansie Cronje took over the captaincy. Wessels has publicly criticised Cronje for the team's performances at times, but by and large the South Africans are a world class team. They have not yet been able to defeat Australia in a series since their return from the wilderness, a fact which still irks most South African players. Wessels felt that they showed a lack of commitment and fight but in reality they are just enjoying their cricket. The fact that they may actually be enjoying playing cricket is lost on people like Wessels.

I feel privileged to have been able to umpire in South Africa but the biggest thrill of all was the opportunity to meet the

President, Nelson Mandela. This great honour was to come during the Cape Town Test against India in January 1997. When he arrived and walked down on to the field I realised why he is held in such high regard. Words almost fail me to describe the feeling of meeting such a great man with a gentle but firm handshake. He took the time to speak with all of the players and I stood waiting with referee Barry Jarman and my umpiring partner, Rudi Koertzen. When it came to my turn his words were 'So you are the man with the most difficult job in cricket'. I wanted to reply with something like 'Not as difficult as your job' but I was spellbound just to be face to face with him.

They are words which I will cherish for the rest of my life because they were spoken with interest, concern and sincerity. I just wish Mr Mandela was a national cricket captain.

CHAPTER THREE

ON ENGLISH WICKETS

I t came as no great surprise to me when Michael Atherton was appointed captain of England. Michael was undoubtedly the man destined to lead England through the nineties with his courage and tenacity. He has long since earned the respect of his opponents. He was no number eight with the bat either. Some of his innings were the best individual performances I have ever seen. He certainly had my respect when he came to the helm.

When Michael took over the reins, England were poised to enter a new era with a seemingly endless string of talented young batsmen and bowlers available for selection. Darren Gough and Dominic Cork were an opening bowling pair capable of removing the top order consistently and others such as Angus Fraser, Chris Lewis and Andy Caddick provided steady back up to apply pressure.

The batting always looked strong with Stewart, Thorpe,

Ramprakash and Hussain. I believed this type of team would always be stiff opposition for whoever they played. When Atherton resigned in Antigua early in 1998, following another series loss to the West Indies, his own form had slipped, yet I still thought he should never be blamed for his team's inability to win. He was an excellent leader who, from my observations, had the full support of his players on the field and that of the England Cricket Board off the field.

It begs the question—are English players being developed to cope with modern international cricket? Having not been involved in English county cricket I am not properly qualified to answer with authority. However in his book, *The Botham Report*, Ian Botham revealed that the emphasis is all on county cricket and little if any thought and preparation is given to progression beyond the English first class scene.

As Botham states, a lot needs to be done to identify, develop and nurture the available talent to supply England with a competitive national team. All focus must ultimately be on playing for your country. I believe English players have the pride in playing for their country but are so stale from the daily grind of the local county scene that it must be nearly impossible to remain sharp and hungry. It seems to me that it's that lack of hunger that you see in players from other countries that prevents England from winning. They simply can't draw the hard and tough men who would die for their cap.

My views on English cricket have not been formed lightly or without much consideration. I have been involved in eight Tests with England which were played in Australia, South Africa, New Zealand and the West Indies. In all I have seen them win four, draw three and lose only one game.

During those matches I have witnessed some remarkable performances, both team and individual, the most notable being
Atherton batting during the second innings in Johannesburg in
1995.

Michael was faced with batting for almost eleven hours
to draw the match and after receiving excellent support from
Robin Smith and Jack Russell he compiled 185 not out in
what I class as the best innings I have seen. I make this judgement, not because it was an aggressive or attacking innings,
but one showing extreme concentration and determination. I
have seen very few players who are capable or willing to play
such an innings and it had world class written all over it.

England also won a game in Christchurch chasing 314 in
the fourth innings to win. After being 7 for 210 it was left to
Cork and Hussain to grind out the required runs which they
did with several overs to spare. Atherton's contribution of 95
odd was not to be dismissed lightly here either.

Another game which England almost collared was in
Sydney in 1994 in fading light when after being set 449 to win,
Australia, after cruising early, had gone to lunch at 0 for 206.
This match saw the emergence of Darren Gough as a world
class all rounder, scoring a whirlwind 50 and taking 6 wickets
for the match. Unfortunately Gough broke down, not long
after, in Melbourne with an ankle injury which was to hinder
his progression for some months. Goughie is now back in
action and under full steam which means headaches for
opposition batsman.

Taylor and Slater both made centuries and with only 243
required in two sessions with a full hand of wickets, Australia
looked likely to pull off one of the greatest wins in history.

Such is the great uncertainty of Test cricket that the after lunch session brought a flood of dismissals which opened the door for England to pull off an unlikely win. Warne and May shared a tense 50 run partnership with England being forced to use spinners in the fading light after Australia had tumbled to be 292 for 7.

The game finished with the usual spotlight on the umpires. Steve Bucknor and I had to rearrange the playing times due to rain breaks and the 'last hour' actually began at 6.26 p.m. with a minimum of fifteen overs to be bowled by 7.26 p.m. Such a strange finishing time is disconcerting, especially when wickets are falling and my concentration was astray when the fifteenth over was completed at 7.21 p.m. Both sides were focused on the bowling of the actual fifteen overs, which, as I have said, is a minimum only, and seemed happy to leave the field. When queried by Mike Atherton, Steve and I then realised that play should actually continue until 7.26 p.m.

The problem was that the ground staff had brought onto the ground tractors with pitch covers, the stumps had been removed, players had shaken hands and almost everyone considered the game to be at a close. I must add here that at no stage did the umpires actually call 'time'. Under the rules of the game play can cease early if both captains are in agreement. This appeared to be what had happened to the untrained eye.

Following a request from Atherton, we thumbed through our notebooks and agreed that there was still time left for play. An interchange of men and machinery was ordered and by the time the ground had been cleared and the stumps reset, the clock read 7.24 p.m. After four balls had been played back to Phil Tufnell and Australia were 7 wickets down England conceded and the match came to a halt for the second and final time.

Had it not been for the rain interruptions Australia may well have been worse off than 7 wickets down at the close.

I was again tagged 'controversial' because of my perceived reluctance to ask for video assistance on decisions. With Australia making a pretty good fist of the chase, Mark Taylor on 78 an hour before lunch, chose to take a third run and when Graham Gooch broke to stumps it was very close but I decided to give Taylor not out.

The replay showed it to be much closer than I had judged it to be in the first instance. In fact there may have been a good case for giving Taylor out depending on which slow motion frame you wanted to use. However Bill Cameron, the third umpire, told me that from what he saw, the benefit would have gone to Taylor had I referred the decision to him. My reluctance to use the available technology got me into considerable trouble and it was not the first time I had been caught out like this.

During an earlier World Series match I had given Grant Flower of Zimbabwe not out in similar fashion but for a far more important Test match. With hindsight, it is fair to say that I had a duty to get things right. Criticism came from everywhere, even resulting in a prominent Australian Cricket Board official 'unofficially' informing the England management that I would not be appointed to any of the remaining Test matches due to my poor form.

I can understand being dropped for that very reason but this sort of thing is very disappointing when it comes from someone who has never umpired a game in his life. This is exactly the sort of situation that gets under an umpire's skin. All National Teams have selectors who are former players and therefore players know if they are not selected they have been dropped by someone who has a reasonable knowledge of first class cricket. Umpires are selected (and dropped) by a selection panel which in every case, including in England, has members who have barely umpired a first class match in their lives. Some sort of equity in umpiring is urgently needed.

In the Taylor incident, England claimed that had Taylor been given out, they would have won the match. This is a simplistic view that I certainly don't subscribe to. I had to accept the criticism however and take it on the chin. The idea of using television technology was introduced to make our job easier and I had been shown up for arriving at a decision by using a certain amount of guesswork and not the facts as they would have been presented on a television replay.

However, the available pictures quite often do not give a definitive answer. South Africa is the only country with cameras in fixed positions at both ends and on either side of the wicket.

The England Cricket Board recently experimented with the same system at Lords but that is the only ground in the country with access to this type of technology. Such limited use of the technology is far from ideal and can only result in inconsistent decisions being given by the third umpire. The reason given for the reluctance of other countries to follow suit is the cost factor, some $200 000 per field. I am yet to be convinced it would not be money well spent. While any slow motion picture is probably better than the naked eye in the heat of the moment it is far from a perfect situation to have a camera mounted in mid-pitch which also takes a sweeping view of the action.

The ICC referee, John Reid, also managed to convince me that umpires are expected to take a commonsense attitude with close decisions. In other words, use the technology or end up looking like a goose. The result has been for umpires to take the safe option and not make the decision ourselves. To my knowledge, umpires throughout the world now have virtually all run out appeals decided off the field much to the dismay of everyone watching when batsmen are found to be yards short of their ground. It is a shame in such circumstances that the human element has been removed—but that's progress.

Michael Atherton's comments were:

> I just think that if the technology is there, umpires may as well use it. It's commonsense, you don't lose anything by using it. It's a fail-safe method. Therefore if run outs are reasonably close, the technology should be used.

It's OK, Michael, I have learned my lesson. I agree.

No cricketer's international career is complete without achieving the dream of playing at Lords. This was realistic for players but never for umpires until the ICC Panel became a reality. The Lords ground holds a certain grandeur and charm that everyone aspires to be part of. So when an invitation came to umpire at the home of cricket, it was also a dream come true for me.

As if not only being asked to officiate at the ground was a big enough thrill, the icing on the cake was that my partner was to be Dickie Bird. It was June 1996 and it was also to be Dickie's final Test match so the honour became even greater. I stood with Dickie in Hobart the previous year and it was a game in which both of us had our share of close decisions to make. We got most right and a few wrong but Dickie was so well respected by the players that it made me feel rather insignificant and my part in the decision making process somewhat immaterial.

It is some understatement that Hobart and Lords are two completely different grounds and I didn't want to start at Lords by asking Dickie how he had enjoyed his time in Hobart. It was not necessary for anyone to ask me how I felt about Lords because to me the place is just awesome and Dickie seemed as pleased as punch that the home of cricket was to be the venue for his final curtain call. The view from the middle looking back towards the members stand is amazing and 'the slope' on the pitch is as I had been told. It is quite pronounced, in fact the whole ground slopes away some nine feet from the western side to the stand on the East.

On the first morning of the Test Michael Atherton had arranged for both teams to give Dickie a guard of honour onto the ground. It was a wonderful gesture by Atherton and made for an emotional entry to the field on the first morning— for me that is, I was not really sure how Dickie felt until we were virtually in the middle. The response from the crowd had been quite amazing and they genuinely loved this man and all the character he brought to the game. They were saying farewell and we hadn't even bowled the first ball yet!

I had volunteered to take the first over to allow Dickie to relax a bit and regain his composure—not that he had ever lost it. Unfortunately, he had already decided he wanted to start at the members' end, and for those who know him well when his mind is made up, nothing is going to change it. Anyway, the breeze was coming from the nursery end so I was sure Srinath would bowl from my end.

The best laid plans quite often come unstuck and this morning was nothing different. Srinath paced out his run up from Dickie's end and began uphill into the wind. I have never really understood fast bowlers even though I was one myself. Anyway, Dickie repaid Atherton for all his help by giving him out LBW in the first over.

People have since asked me if Dickie still had misty eyes when he gave the decision. He didn't, of course, as he was the complete professional and when the first ball was bowled, he was as ready as he had been for his previous sixty-five Tests.

One of Dickie's habits is that he is inclined to leave you behind if you don't keep a pace with him. When he decides it's time to go off and start the game he is off like a shot out of a cannon. Lords is not a good place for a stranger to get lost and the umpires' room is situated up three flights of stairs and around the inside of a grand old building. I judiciously follow-ed either Dickie or Alan Whitehead who was the third umpire whenever we had to climb these stairs.

Another trait that Dickie possesses is that he always leaves things to the absolute last minute and it does take some three minutes to get from the umpires' room, down the stairs and through the Long Room before reaching the ground. After the tea break on day two, Dickie after all his fidgeting and checking of gear, decided to speed off without much notice.

In trying to follow him I was distracted by an expatriate Aussie wishing me well when all of a sudden Dickie was out of sight. I raced down the stairs at breakneck speed (for me), out of the door only to be confronted by members picnicking on the lawn at the back of the stand. In my haste I had gone one flight of stairs too many.

The steward quickly pointed me in the right direction, back up and through the Long Room and there was Dickie waiting with hands on hips saying, 'There's a good chap, Darrell, hurry on we can't keep them waiting, can we?' It has always been my worst nightmare to actually be last onto the field but we managed to whiz down the stairs just in front of the players.

Prior to the Lords game I had been appointed to the Edgbaston Test with David Shepherd. I had been lucky to have as partners two of the best umpires in the world. It doesn't matter though who your partner is as on some occasions things just will not go as planned. The Edgbaston Test was won by England quite easily by 8 wickets but that did not stop the old cry of 'We were robbed' from the losers.

India cited two of my decisions as being biased and incompetent. These comments were made by a high ranking Indian Cricket Board official who also labelled me a racist. He later denied he had made that claim but did not retract the accusations of incompetence and bias. It is always disappointing when these statements appear in the press as I fear fans who were not at the ground probably accept them as fact.

The first of the disputed decisions came when I rejected an appeal for a catch by the keeper. Nasser Hussain was batting and Srinath was bowling around the wicket. A shortish delivery went down the leg side resulting in a huge appeal, for a catch. It was a difficult one as I had heard no noise at all and there was no deflection that I could pick up. Hussain's gloves were close to the ball as it sailed past but I decided on a not out call.

I have never seen a replay but from all reports it does not definitely show contact with the glove so I believed the benefit had been rightly given to the batsman. To make matters worse (much worse) Hussain was only about fifteen at the time and of course went on to score a century. This effectively shut India out of any chance of winning.

On the other side of the coin, had I given Hussain out on less than convincing evidence, it would have only been a rough guess and may have even cost him his place in the team. I will never know the truth but worrying about it is something I tend not to do. You can't go over and over these things or you wouldn't be able to do the job.

The other decision which caused something of a drama was a catch by Graham Hick at second slip. Hick claimed a low catch off Rathore who stood his ground as he was perfectly entitled to do. I was not sure the ball had carried which is quite often the dilemma for the umpire at the bowler's end. I asked David Shepherd for his opinion and he believed the ball had been fairly caught. I then gave Rathore out.

What followed was a succession of television replays which were inconclusive from all angles. The matter was about to be put to rest when a final camera angle replay showed the ball had fractionally touched the grass in front of Hick. I will always have to accept the blame for decisions within my jurisdiction and I in no way hold Shepherd responsible as he could only tell me what he had seen. The final decision was always going to be mine.

Unfortunately, I gained the tag 'incompetent' even though it was a decision made in good faith. What most people had forgotten is that the fieldsman claiming this type of catch must know in his heart whether he has completed a fair catch. I have never confronted Hick about this incident but it was probably one used in evidence in the case for use of television replays to decide if a catch has been clearly and fairly taken.

We are now using the technology for catches a procedure which was included in the ICC regulations last season. I wonder how the players now feel about trying to claim catches? It is a sad reflection on the game that we cannot trust the players to compete with the spirit in which the game is supposed to be played.

The life of an international cricket umpire can sometimes drive you to distraction through frustration due to the uncertainty about when, or indeed, if, your next appointment will ever arrive. We umpires on the ICC panel usually get about six to eight weeks' notice of appointment for Test matches and after the end of the Australian summer I was not due to umpire any of the upcoming Tests during the South African tour of England.

The ICC had scheduled the International Umpires Conference for July so I decided to travel to England early with the hope of picking up some minor games in the local leagues. I had always wanted to spend a summer in England to enjoy the sights of the English countryside and maybe even a few of the special ales on tap. During my previous visit in 1996 when I umpired two matches, there had been barely enough time to finish the Test matches and before I had to return home to Australia.

In an effort to learn more about the game, I contacted the MCC and the European Cricket Council (ECC) to see if they could arrange some umpiring appointments where I may have been able to be of some assistance with the development of local umpiring. I was staggered by the response. I was made an 'Honorary ECC Umpiring Instructor' and sent on trips to Italy, Malta and Ireland.

This sort of program is not available in Australia and the opportunity to assist with the umpire development in the other countries made the trip very worthwhile. I think more countries should follow the lead of the European Cricket Council and make good use of the International umpires in promotional roles. It does seem strange that an umpire can be sent twelve thousand miles to umpire just one game when there are plenty of other opportunities to make full use of his experience in training and development.

While the standard of cricket in Italy and Malta may not be anywhere near first class, there is enthusiasm and commitment among the players although they rely fairly heavily on ex-patriots. Matches are played on artificial turf but this in no way diminishes the passion with which the game is played. The umpiring needs to be improved considerably and the ECC is taking the right steps to ensure that resources for umpiring are at least commensurate with those for the player development. Umpiring has to be of an acceptable standard or the game falls into decline. Cricketers at all levels feel disappointment that their day can often be spoiled by substandard umpiring.

The icing on the cake however, was a call from ICC with a late invitation to umpire the Test at Lords. I thought about it for all of five seconds before accepting. Another match at the very seat of the game after umpiring there in 1996 was a great thrill and certainly kept my adrenalin pumping.

South Africa were to run out what seemed like easy winners but not before they had experienced their own slice of luck at various stages. Having been sent in to bat by Alec Stewart, South Africa at one stage were 4 for 50 and would have been 5 for 50 if Mike Atherton had accepted a sharp chance at third slip off Jonty Rhodes. The chance went begging and Jonty went on to score a well deserved century out of a total of 370. England were then bowled out cheaply and after following on they again collapsed. South Africa had to score just 15 runs to win by 10 wickets.

I ended up in the news again as a result of a decision given against Mark Ramprakash in the first innings. With England fighting hard to avoid the follow on, Alan Donald sent down one of his trademark thunderbolts which jagged back sharply to take what I thought was a clear inside edge.

Boucher took the 'catch' and much to the annoyance of Ramprakash, I gave him out.

What Mark said to me on his way from the crease was something which I found to be totally unacceptable as an umpire. He said, 'You must enjoy destroying careers like mine', the inference behind such a comment is that an umpire has had a pre-meditated plan to give a batsmen out. This is utter nonsense and was a comment I was not prepared to accept in any form of cricket.

The hearing conducted later by Javed Burki, the ICC referee, left Mark in no doubt that he had erred in a serious way not just because of what he said but the fact that the whole incident had been caught by the television cameras and replayed over and over again. The sight of a player obviously mouthing off to an umpire is not the image that cricket should be portaying to the millions of youngsters watching on TV. If such a high profile player is allowed to get away with such indiscretions, then it is a clear signal to others that it is acceptable to carry on in this way.

Ramprakash was fined £800 and given a suspended sentence of one Test match which was a penalty consistent with his good record in the past. I cannot help feeling that instances such as this will continue to occur until some player is suspended for one or two Test matches. Only then will players know that there are serious consequences if they misbehave and it would also send a message to all youngsters that the umpires are there to be respected not abused when they make decisions with which some players do not agree.

Of course, the multitude of television replays did in fact show that I had given Ramrakash out incorrectly as the ball had actually grazed his elbow on the way through. I have no drama with the truth being found but I was only giving a decision based on what I thought I had seen and heard.

Hopefully we umpires can continue to learn from our mistakes the same way that a player has to work on a flaw in his technique. I know that I will never stop learning on and off the field.

Contrary to some reports, Mark and I continue to get on well and he made the time and effort to talk to me when he was batting in the second innings. Talking to players is not something I usually instigate as I realise they have a routine to follow so they can concentrate especially when batting and I appreciated Mark's gesture. We even shared a drink later on in the series during the Fourth Test at Trent Bridge. I think he realises his choice of words was poor but my opinion of him as a player has not been affected in any way. I still rate him as being one of the best batsmen in England and a man who can be relied upon in a crisis. I just hope that I get the next decision 100 per cent correct when we meet again on the field.

Because of this incident at Lords, media coverage of the series became more intense and the umpires in the next three Tests were under incredible scrutiny. Every decision they made was dissected and analysed until things finally were blown right out of proportion during the Fourth Test at Trent Bridge. Merv Kitchen and Steve Dunne had a difficult time with a couple of decisions, but now that the series was in the balance after England had salvaged a draw at Old Trafford, both teams were playing tough and hard with no apologies.

There has already been a lot of comment over the years about the reluctance of batsmen to 'walk' when they know they are out. Also there was the constant appealing by bowlers and wicket keepers when they knew the batsman was not out. Some commentators eventually alleged that such behaviour by players constituted cheating and this all came to a head when Michael Atherton refused to 'walk' after an appeal for a catch behind. Umpire Steve Dunne had decided the ball came off Atherton's forearm much to the disgust of the South Africans.

So Steve and I both ruled incorrectly during this series and on one occasion the batsman was accused of cheating for not walking when he did get a glove on it, and the other occasion (mine) the bowling side copped a blast for appealing when it wasn't out. In my opinion neither of these instances constitutes cheating.

I find it difficult to level an allegation of cheating as what may seem clearly not out to me as an umpire may genuinely appear to be definitely out to the fielding side. This happens all the time. The bowlers are entitled to appeal under the laws of the game and indeed, a batsman cannot be given out unless there is an appeal. I have always taken the view that once an appeal is made and ruled on, the game must proceed without dissent. If this happens I have no problem with there being a thousand appeals providing that if I say not out a thousand times the game continues without further on field conjecture. This does put me at odds with some of the other ICC umpires such as Steve Bucknor and Peter Willey who have openly stated that players are indeed cheating in many of these instances.

There were many other exciting moments in the series that were largely overlooked due to the controversies about umpiring decisions. The batting of Gough, Croft and Fraser was nail-biting stuff as they enabled England to salvage a draw at Old Trafford. The performances of Fraser taking another 10 wicket haul and Atherton repelling a volatile Alan Donald at Trent Bridge is what Test matches are all about. Donald's bowling bears special mention for sheer ferocity but also for the fact that he might have gone too far, a matter largely forgotten in the heat of the battle. The question is 'was this type of bowling in contravention of Law 42.8?'

The wording of the law states that:

The bowling of fast short pitched balls is unfair if in the opinion of the umpire at the bowler's end that by their repetition and taking into account their length, height and direction, they are likely to inflict physical injury on the striker, irrespective of the protective clothing and equipment he may be wearing. The relative skill of the striker shall also be taken into consideration. In the event of such unfair bowling, the umpire shall adopt the procedure of cautioning and no balling the bowler.

The bowler is then removed from the attack after three such calls.

This law gives the umpire considerable powers but he also has to make a judgement about the relative skill of the batsman. In Atherton's case, there can be no doubt about his skill and ability to play such deliveries but there are other batsmen around the world who bat in the top order who are completely incapable of handling this type of bowling. Most players who play Test cricket accept the fact that they are going to have a ball released in their direction at around 90 miles per hour and the general feeling is that they will have to withstand such an onslaught if they are to prove their worth at the top level.

Intimidated or not, the England batsmen were sporting a fair few bruises and the evasive action being taken indicates that they were indeed in danger of serious physical injury. What also made Donald's onslaught more intimidating was his decision to bowl around the wicket having failed to win the battle from the more orthodox angle. The positioning of fieldsmen on the leg-side also gives a reasonable insight into the plan he was employing.

The ICC playing conditions for Test matches allow only two fast short pitched balls per over which pass above shoulder height but in most cases it is not the ball sailing way over the head of a batsman which causes the drama. It is the ball directed into the ribs which is the intimidating aspect. That is when Law 42.8 comes into play.

You don't have to be a genius to know that the main purpose of going around the wicket is to narrow the angle and make it more difficult for the batsmen to avoid the bouncers. The only justification is to increase the chances of a slips catch or a bat pad to the close in-fielder. Unless a batsman is completely inept he should never be bowled in this situation and the angle completely precludes any LBW decision going in the bowler's favour.

So, should umpires intervene in such situations at Test match level? If we do, people will say we are ruining a contest at the ultimate level where batsman and bowler are expected to perform to the highest standards and to win the battle by being mentally and physically stronger than the opponent. If we do not, what sort of message are we sending to all other levels of cricket? My belief in the instance of Atherton and Donald is that while the fine line was probably crossed, the relative skill of Atherton was sufficient to allow it to continue. Had it been to a lesser skilled man then there is no question that the bowling would be out of order and should be stopped immediately.

The application of the law at other levels of cricket should follow a stricter interpretation but umpires must be aware of other problems such as the following scenario. Imagine an aging fast bowler in club cricket making a desperate effort to win a game for his team. He knows all the tricks and goes around the wicket to bowl short and fast directly at the batsman. Unfortunately he has lost some pace and fitness and is hit for boundary after boundary by a gleeful batsman. At the other end though is a young bowler who has no problem sending a succession of short pitched deliveries into the ribs and helmet of the same batsman who is now clearly in danger of suffering serious physical injury.

Under the current laws the umpires should act immediately by invoking Law 42.8 against the young fast bowler only. The aging bowler is not causing any danger and under the wording of the law is not likely to inflict serious physical injury.

CHAPTER FOUR

THE CRICKET WORLD'S BEST KEPT SECRET —SHEFFIELD SHIELD

There can be no doubt whatsoever that the Sheffield Shield competition is the ultimate breeding ground for the world's best cricketers. It is the only cricket competition around the globe which is openly envied by other countries. Imran Khan, the former captain of Pakistan, when playing a season with New South Wales during the eighties, made the comment that the Sheffield Shield was 'the world's best kept secret'.

Imran, like many others from overseas who have had the opportunity to play here, are in awe of the toughness, intensity and competitiveness of Shield cricket. There are no easy runs or wickets to be scored or taken. A young player gains practised skills and knowledge about fitness, both mental and physical. This goes a long way towards explaining why, when a young player is picked to play for Australia, he is ready in every way for this new and ultimate challenge.

It has, however, become all too clear that the competition is a serious drain on resources due to various circumstances such as the long distances travelled for some matches. I have no doubt the Australian Cricket Board would not be tempted to radically tamper with such a success story. I refer to success in terms of results the national team has achieved at Test match level even though the performances at One Day level have fallen away somewhat.

To digress for a moment, what needs to be recognised with regard to the one day game is that other countries have improved and adapted to the shorter form and have been able to pick up some rather soft wins against the Australians. Test matches, however, should always be the gauge of true ability and Australia has a very formidable record apart from a recent series loss to India.

The Australian Cricket Board have decided on a policy picking separate teams for the one day game which may go a long way towards securing greater success in the future. I have no set view on the concept other than to say that there is sufficient talent available from which to pick the two teams and it may in fact go a long way towards prolonging the careers of the Test players. The number and extent of injuries being suffered by the top line players should be ample proof that longer rest periods are required.

So, back to the domestic competition—why then is cricket played in such a do or die fashion where only the talented and strong succeed? I believe that the pride and tradition of playing for the state cap is seen by players as being the culmination of years of hard work and their talent has been duly recognised. I have heard them say things like 'It doesn't get any better than this'. But after a few games they gain confidence and eye off a team mate who has worn the baggy green cap and they set their sights on that new goal. They know they are only one step away from that dream.

The tradition associated with the Sheffield Shield makes it a winner on one level but there have been alarm bells ringing for some time. Many sections of the media believe the game will not progress unless the crowds can be lured back to the grounds. Because crowds have become so low some states are putting on promotions such as 'dollar days' in an attempt to attract more through the gate. Each state has a marketing department in place to gain a larger share of the corporate dollar to better support their teams.

Day/night matches have been scheduled to appeal to the families with limited time available at weekends. These measures, while worth trying, have not been successful in attracting crowds to the grounds. It is such a shame. Although cricket has more atmosphere when played before sell-out crowds, I don't think large numbers of spectators are achievable at Sheffield Shield level in today's financial climate and with the increasingly busier and more diverse lifestyles of the Australian public. It is, of course desirable to draw greater crowds but in the wash-up it has no effect on the hunger of the players to achieve and excel and progress to the next level.

There is so much cricket played and televised that the public see no reason to go along and watch the very competition which supplies them with their heroes in Test matches. The fact that Pay Television has recently taken up the rights to telecast selected matches will only benefit the game and hopefully bring it to the attention of the public again.

The Sheffield Shield competition also has a role to play in the development of umpires and for most of the reasons I have already mentioned, it is a tough stage on which to perform. Quite often an umpire's decision can have a big bearing on a player's future but some players and captains have only been too quick to lay the blame fairly and squarely on the umpires when things don't go according to their plans and hopes.

How an umpire handles the tough situations will determine how successful he will be in the long run. It is very intense pressure when players are agitated with their form and with you but no matter how upset they are, the umpire must be able to show people that what we do is for the good of the game. It also depends on how far things are let go. If, for example, a player is just voicing his opinion on a decision, he is perfectly entitled to do so. People are human.

If a bad call is made it may be best for the umpire to admit his mistake by saying something like 'we all make mistakes but it's not intentional'. Players will then feel like you are dealing with them with fairness rather than malice. But if they become abusive or try to show you up as a poor decision maker or question your integrity or fairness then it's time to take control by insisting there be no more abuse. Of course, in that situation we will never win any popularity contests.

The major problem facing umpires at first class level seems to be a lack of acceptance of umpires who have never played the game at their level. This was confirmed in a players' poll conducted by *Inside Edge* magazine when the question was asked, 'What is the major problem with umpiring?' The answer was 'not enough have played first class cricket. This to me is a fair enough response when you consider that the Shield teams almost always have a coach and development staff who are former Shield players. They are dealing with people who have played at their level in most other areas of their game.

The problem is that when the recruitment classes come along each year, there are never any retired players who are willing to commit to an umpiring career. This to me is not an umpiring development problem, it is a world cricket dilemma. There are exceptions in the English system where all umpires are former county players but the only other country that has a Test player umpiring is India where Venkat has been a great success. It seems the world cricket authorities need to make umpiring a viable career path and then we may have some success in recruitment.

The Sheffield Shield holds many fine memories for me. It became obvious in my playing days with North Sydney and later Mosman that I would not be gracing the cricket grounds of Australia as a representative player. I was capable of filling a place in first grade but not as a regular. After representing NSW Schoolboys under 14 years and later Western District (NSW) Colts teams, my time as a player was notable for being unremarkable. The lure of beer gardens, warm beaches and night life had a considerable effect on my attitude to training and fitness and therefore any playing potential I may have had unfortunately never surfaced. So as the 'demon' fast deliveries began being flayed to and over the fence, thoughts of my walking on to the SCG were consigned to the realms of fantasy.

I retired from playing at the conclusion of the 1983 season. A succession of knee injuries requiring surgery made the decision easy. My doctor at the time informed me that should I continue playing, incisions of a major nature would be required. Not wanting to spend weeks on crutches, (not to mention the minor matter of being allergic to pain) I thought retirement was a good option. After a brief time terrorising the bookies at Randwick with no success at all I was lured back to the game that had been my love for as far back as I could remember.

In short, I took up umpiring. Friends gave me those strange looks that make you think you have just contracted leprosy. I was happy though (and had much more money in my pockets) and I began umpiring the local Sydney fourth grade competition which gave me enormous satisfaction.

A rather rapid advance through the lower grade ranks alerted me to the possibility of umpiring at first class level so much so that when I was elevated to the Sydney first grade panel I immediately set a goal to reach Sheffield Shield cricket. I wanted to walk onto the Sydney Cricket Ground by reaching the the top of my new and very much chosen profession. I had never before had such a passionate goal and I was determined not to let this chance slip by.

I endured almost two full seasons in first grade, interspersed with minor representative games at Colts and Second Eleven level before the opportunity came and the New South Wales versus Tasmania Sheffield Shield fixture came out with my name attached to it in February 1989. I will forever cherish the day and remember with pride walking down the steps and out onto the hallowed turf of that famous ground with my good friend Ian Thomas to make my debut. I had no idea how far I would go in umpiring but I felt I had 'arrived'.

There may be some truth in the old story about being in the right place at the right time as the recent retirements of Dick French and Rocky Harris from the ranks of New South Wales umpires had left an opening or two. Ross Emerson and Trevor Jay were departures interstate which opened the door a little wider.

Tasmania were captained by Dirk Wellham and Geoff Lawson was in command of the New South Wales team. The match proved a fairly tough one to umpire but thankfully Lawson and Wellham had so much unfinished business to square off they left the umpires pretty much alone to do our job. I quickly realised that both captains had not forgotten past differences and some fiery exchanges took place, none of which can be printed here.

I learned from this game that the players treated everything in such a tough, uncompromising and fully professional manner that the learning curve for umpires needed to be acute and immediate if we were to survive. My partner Ian Thomas already had some exposure to this type of cricket and I recall him saying to me, 'That was about as tough and tense as it gets out there'. I was to find out later in my career that it does get tougher but only by a whisker or two.

Despite my enthusiasm and dedication, umpiring to me until then had still been a pastime and I will not ever forget that very little was done to prepare and train an umpire for this level of cricket. It was very much a suck it and see, trial and error brief. Or more succinctly, sink or swim. That was ten years ago and thankfully, more attention is now given to the development of umpires but there is still much to be done to ensure the game has a continual flow of competent umpires.

I can now look back on ten years and thirty-five Sheffield Shield encounters, including six finals, to see that it was not always plain sailing and the thought 'you are only as good as your last game' still holds true today. Naturally umpires make mistakes and I have made my share, some will even say more that my share, and quite rightly so.

In a four or five day match, an umpire is expected to be as fresh and alert on the last day as he was on day one. You don't have to be genius to realise that this is not humanly possible. What is possible and expected is that mistakes or errors of judgement will be kept to an absolute minimum. Players are forgiven for the odd mistake whether it be a missed catch or an ill-judged attempt for an extra run. They will not be dropped from the team if they prove that their potential and their talent has not diminished. Players are even allowed quite long periods of poor form.

The same tolerance should be accorded to umpires providing the mistakes don't turn in to an avalanche of poor judgement. Umpires get tired and fatigued in the same way players do so the odd lapse in concentration levels and intensity is bound to occur. The better class umpires, the same as the better class players will keep them to an absolute minimum. To call or play the perfect game would be ideal but in reality it will never be possible.

Some decisions I have made have been proved to be wrong but if I can learn from them, there is a basis for improved performance. Umpires have to learn to accept criticism and I will list a few (not all) of the decisions I have made for which I would love to be able to turn back the clock and call them again.

The first for mention may have had a considerable effect on the outcome of the game and it happened to be a Shield Final involving New South Wales and Tasmania in 1994. Rod Tucker the Tasmanian captain was batting and Tasmania were making a middle order recovery when a quick single turned into a nightmare for me when I gave Tucker out, run out. All of my senses deserted me at the time and for some silly and unexplained reason, I gave him out. Whilst it was a close decision, I should have given Tucker the benefit of the doubt but that was not what I did.

With hindsight Rod had probably made his ground and a photograph in the daily newspapers the next day did not show my decision in a particularly good light. The annoying thing for me was that we were operating under a rotating system of three umpires whereby one umpire was having a rest for a session at a time. This system had been instigated by the Australian Cricket Board on a trial basis to ensure umpires were not subject to fatigue. In principle, the system had good foundations and intentions but it also denied the umpire any continuity and actually broke my routine and concentration. It was simple to sit out the first or last session of the day but having a break from lunchtime (1.00 p.m.) until resumption of play after the tea break (4.00 p.m.) made it just about impossible to get back on track straight away. Also the constant change of ends didn't help either.

Steven Waugh was to make the comment that by having three umpires it was difficult to obtain consistency from one session to another. He also said there was a 33 per cent chance of more mistakes, a comment which I found most amusing. Bowlers had trouble with what they perceived to be a plumb

LBW given not out in the first session and obligingly given out in the last session. Some batsmen were also confounded for obvious reasons.

That was no reason for getting the Tucker decision wrong but what it did do was cause a lot of ill feeling between Tasmanian cricketers and myself which has taken some time to remedy. My partners in that game were Steve Randell and Terry Prue and most would say that the wealth of experience between us should be enough to ensure a trouble-free game. Unfortunately, it was me that let the team down and I should never have allowed that to happen.

New South Wales went on to win the game but I will never know if that particular decision did deprive Tasmania of their maiden Shield title. Rod Tucker is still performing well for Tasmania and we still meet up now and then during the course of a season. I know that Rod was less than compliment- ary in his captain's report about my umpiring performance but to this day we have never mentioned the subject to each other in conversation. I guess that cricketers and umpires really just want to get on with their respective jobs and enjoy their cricket.

The next two incidents both involved Queensland and thankfully did not affect the result as Queensland went on to win both games. In Brisbane during early 1996, I gave Adam Dale out caught behind when replays showed the ball quite clearly making contact with the thigh pad. If that was not bad enough, I repeated the error in the Shield Final in Perth during the same season. That time Geoff Foley was the unlucky batsman.

On both occasions, the batsmen were left-handers with a

right arm bowler coming from around the wicket. This situation creates a dilemma for umpires as the ball is continually slanted across the batsmen. The angle is not good and if umpires stood at mid-off then the decisions would be much easier. We cannot take that position of course and have to do the best we can. I assure you it is not at all easy.

The hardest decision of all is the bat/pad situation. Quite often a lot of noises appear to come from the other end of the pitch and most of it is definitely not the result of contact with the bat or glove. Fieldsmen themselves are not sure and the temptation to appeal when any sort of noise is heard is understandable. I have found the best answer is not to guess. Sometimes the view of the umpire and the players is poles apart.

CHAPTER FIVE

THE BRAVE NEW WORLD OF INDEPENDENT AND TELEVISION UMPIRES

The announcement by the International Cricket Council in 1994 that an independent panel of umpires would be formed to officiate in all Test matches caused much debate. It seemed that there were equal umbers for and against the concept. The umpiring world in general was aggrieved at the use of the terms 'independent' and 'neutral' considering that the reason for having umpires in the game in the first place was that we were, in effect, removed from association with either team so that no favouritism or bias would arise. We were already independent and neutral.

The world, however, is an interesting place and cricket is played in different styles depending on which continent or island you are on. Before the ICC system, most touring teams would return home after a long and arduous tour with complaints that biased or incompetent umpiring had cost them a win. There was, however, no emerging pattern of where the best or worst umpires came from. Still players' perceptions persisted that they would be shafted somewhere, sometime and probably at a crucial stage of a tour.

When England toured Australia in the early seventies they were generally critical of the umpires here but especially the failure to give LBW decisions. It transpires that only two Australian batsmen were given out in this manner and the captain at the time was not one of them. England were also to complain about umpires on tours of Pakistan and India and to the surprise of no-one Pakistan would lodge complaints when touring England and Australia. Where would it all end and what was the solution?

The cricket world has always accepted that English umpires are the best in the world because they are the only full time professional body of umpires operating. Nearly all on the England panel were former first class county players and their knowledge and experience of cricket cannot be under-estimated. There are no arguments from me on that basis, but umpires should not be crucified just because they are not able to be full time professionals or, in other words, because the system operated by their home cricket board does not embrace the English concept.

When the ICC announced the format of the initial panel, there were to be two umpires from each Test-playing country and four from England. The umpires were not selected by ICC but came from nominations by each country. These nominations were unconditionally accepted and formed the panel which was reviewed each year but changes were only made at the request of each country.

The knockers of the system complained that the best

umpires may still not emerge but I think the system was the best option open to ICC at that time. The negative side of the system was that only one independent umpire would be appointed for each Test match which still left the door open for criticism of the 'local' appointee. The idea, however, had the major benefit of helping to eliminate the perceived bias and it did not throw two umpires into a game in a foreign country that they had never previously visited. Potential factors like different climates, grounds and facilities were overcome by the local umpire being able to advise and help out with travel to and from the grounds and with general assistance with local customs.

I know for a fact that had I been appointed to a match in a country where I had no knowledge of the language or customs, it would have been a daunting prospect. By and large the system has worked well and the other benefit has been the sharing of information on law interpretations and techniques which otherwise would not have been possible. I think it has seen a rise in the standard of world umpiring but there is still much to be done to improve and refine the umpiring system.

The ICC has been staging an International Umpires' Conference every two years where problems have been raised and tackled. These include the varying interpretations about topics such as unfair play. It is also a commitment by the ICC to show that umpires are serious about their trade and are doing as much as possible to improve their skills and consistency.

I have had ten appointments as the 'neutral' umpire and while I have enjoyed the experience of visiting England, the Caribbean and South Africa there is also a down side to such a system. I am referring to the development of local umpires which stems from the insistence that an ICC panel member would be appointed as the 'local' umpire whenever and wherever possible.

This has had the desired effect of having the best available umpires appointed to each Test match but at what cost? There are only very limited opportunities now for a first class umpire to reach Test level. With umpiring being only a part-time occupation in every country except England, it is becoming increasingly difficult to retain people with talent when they see their chances of becoming a regular Test umpire diminishing.

Recruitment of quality umpires is difficult enough at the moment and maybe it's time to take the plunge and offer umpires a fully professional career path in the game on the same lines as what is being done for players with talent identification from school age. Academies are available for the players who are able to make a virtual full time commitment to the game when first class status has been achieved.

Umpires are usually beginning their career when others have finished playing the game. This is the major contributing difficulty in the recruitment and retention of quality umpires. It is a difficult time in life to be channelling enormous amounts of time and energy into a profession with little prospect of a full-time job.

The other major change to cricket came with the assistance of the use of television replays to decide on close run outs or stumpings. In the past, many decisions which had been made through the umpire's eyes where shown up as incorrect on replays. Nearly always, it was a decision given not out when, in fact, the batsman was a couple of inches short of his ground.

These decisions had gone in favour of the batsman for two hundred years in accordance with the law which states that if there is any doubt, the decision shall be not out. This all changed dramatically with the introduction of the controversial third umpire. Theoretically, there should be no such thing as a lucky escape, but that has not been the case in even recent times.

A large number of instances have arisen necessitating a 'not out' decision because of a poor picture quality or indeed, no picture at all. Human error has now been passed on from the umpire to television personnel. I don't blame the camera operator but more so the procedure for using the third umpire.

Having a quality cameraman is one thing but they cannot be expected to follow a ball travelling at 90 miles an hour and maintain a steady hand so that when the crucial moment arrives the image is not blurred. The answer, of course, is to have dedicated cameras at each end and either side of the stumps.

South Africa has managed such a system through sponsorship but so far they are the only country to have implemented these foolproof cameras. Until such time as each country finds the resources to emulate the South African system we will continue to have contentious decisions being made.

Run outs and stumpings were only the thin edge of the wedge as far as video was concerned. Next came the use for hit wicket decisions. These are also decisions that we umpires are likely to miss. The action quite often happens after the ball has been played but is a fairly rare occurrence.

There are always exceptions, of course, such as last

season. I am referring to the Mark Waugh decision in Adelaide when Mark may or may not have completed his stroke when his bat dislodged the bails. It happened at a crucial time when a Test match was in the balance. This particular instance when Mark knocked the bails is distorted when shown in slow motion. The crucial point or moment is when the batsman actually completes his attempt to play at the ball. There is no way that a frame by frame view of this action can always deliver the correct verdict. In this particular case I believe it showed Mark had finished his stroke and was walking in the direction of leg slip.

Umpires around the world differed in their opinion on the Mark Waugh decision but I back the 'not out' verdict simply because Mark, in my opinion, had definitely completed his stroke. He had been hit on the arm and was walking in the opposite direction when his bat dislodged the bails. South Africans were unanimous that he was out. Even my good friend Cyril Mitchley who was on the ICC panel stated publicly that it should have been out.

All this goes to prove is that there is still a difference in interpretation on vital points of the laws from around the world. When things are taken out of the hands of the men in the middle and placed in the realm of the cameras all sorts of strange things can happen.

The use of video has now been approved to assist with boundary line decisions and whether a catch has been cleanly taken. These two points of law are the most contentious because the incidence of fieldsmen stepping on boundary lines and ropes has increased dramatically as has the 'claiming' of a catch. Umpires are very rarely able to tell from a distance of

80 yards if a foot touches a line. Catches are also particularly difficult to call in the slips region as the ball is usually travelling fast and low to the ground.

Cricket is the gentleman's game but there are instances of certain players being less than honest. We now have the video to call on but the chances of getting a really clear picture on some catches is minuscule. It's such a shame that the game has been forced to include catches and boundaries as part of its technological surveillance of possible cheating.

Another noteworthy aspect of the modern game is the apparent attempt to gain a decision by excessive appealing. This is regularly done and accepted by all national teams as a means of getting their 'fair share' of decisions however incorrect they may be. Pressuring umpires with this type of appealing is such a commonplace event that until recently I had paid little or no attention to it.

It was only after the ICC Umpires' Conference in London this year that I realised how passionate some of the panel umpires were in their insistence that the practice should be stamped out. When respected umpires such as Steve Bucknor, Venkatarahgavan and Peter Willey spoke publicly of their concerns and even used the term 'cheating' it sparked no small amount of controversy about the steps players were willing to take in the name of winning.

I have always had a personal view that players are entitled to appeal as much as they wish provided that when a decision is given against them they must immediately get on with the game and not display petulance and ongoing dissent. This is the way it has always been in Australia and I find it difficult to describe most appeals as being a blatant attempt to cheat. Appealing for a 'catch' when the ball comes off the arm or pad is not cheating as on most occasions the bowler, fielder or wicket keeper is not sure exactly what happened. They will quite often have three different opinions among themselves so it is surely acceptable to call for the umpire's decision. After all, the laws of the game give the right of appeal to the fielding side and a batsman cannot be given out unless there is an appeal.

What I consider to be cheating is trying to influence an umpire by indicating that something did actually happen when, in fact, something completely different has clearly occurred. This type of appeal however is fully covered by the law that the umpire's decision is final and also that we are the sole judges of fair and unfair play. If a player is attempting to cheat, then surely a simple not out answer and a word to the captain should be sufficient to stamp out the practice. The captains are continually being reminded that they are responsible for the game being played in the right spirit.

To say that only the fielding side are guilty of attempted cheating is also not correct. When a batsman immediately rubs his arm after he has gloved a catch is also a blatant cheating tactic aimed at convincing an umpire that something completely different has happened. Waving a bat around when an LBW appeal is made as an attempt to indicate he has hit the ball first is also unforgivable.

Again, the best way to stamp out these unsatisfactory practices must rest with the captains and their responsibilities to uphold the spirit of the game. If they are incapable of doing so, and there are some captains who fit snugly into this category, then the controlling bodies in each country should be encouraged to take swift action to remedy the situation. Imagine how long the excessive and unfair appealing would continue if the captain of the side were to be disciplined or even suspended for failing to ensure the game was played in the correct spirit.

CHAPTER SIX

MY WORLD TEAM

Everyone has a view on who is the best batsmen, bowler or wicket keeper in the world. Sometimes they judge the best by pure statistics over a given period or by standings published by experts who take into account all sorts of elements like home and away performances or runs to balls faced ratios.

The problem with statistics and ratings is that cricketers are not machines and should not be judged by mechanical criteria. I have seen some performances in Sheffield Shield and One Day International games which are pure class and excitement but in compiling my World Eleven I have decided to pick the players only from the Test matches and Sheffield Shield matches in which I have stood. These performances sometimes are not all that easy to evaluate but I consider each player here to have done something special.

This limits the available field and some selections will be

surprising to most avid cricket fans, especially those from Australia. But for what it's worth here is my team and the reasons behind the selections.

OPENING BATSMEN

Michael Atherton

Atherton wins top spot mainly due to his courageous innings of 185 not out against South Africa. Without his determination, England would have lost in four days. This was truly a backs-to-the-wall fighting innings which while not always entertaining was an absolute gem. Michael also showed his true colours again in England in 1998 against South Africa which ensured England were not to be humiliated in another home series. His innings of 98 not out to help England win the Trent Bridge Test must surely have been his best ever performance.

Sachin Tendulkar

Sachin gets the other spot because of his ability to blow away the best bowlers in the world. I realise he does not open for India in Test matches but in a team such as this, he is a perfect foil for Atherton and no doubt would adapt perfectly to the job. Tendulkar is equally at ease against pace or spin on all types of pitches and he picks up the flight of the ball so quickly out of the bowler's hand that he is a bowler's worst nightmare. Shane Warne was on the receiving end of an almighty battering in India and said that Tendulkar must be another Bradman. High praise indeed.

NUMBER THREE

Brian Lara

Brian is the only one I have considered for the number three spot. He can ravage a bowler from the first ball he faces and is equally formidable against speed or spin. His detractors find fault with his high and extravagant backlift but it has never been a bar to him scoring runs. Anyone who can amass huge scores such as double and triple centuries in Test matches has all the attributes and I don't think there is a bowler in the world who would say he looks forward to bowling to Lara. His form of late has not been up to his usual standards but he is still the best player I have umpired so far. A world record score of 375 guarantees him the Number three spot.

NUMBER FOUR

Mark Waugh

Mark has long been considered a cricketer who never takes the game too seriously. I find nothing wrong with that type of attitude but I know for certain that Mark is always annoyed at losing his wicket in what commentators say is a 'soft' way. He seems to enjoy batting so much that it is impossible for me to agree with the critics. After all why get yourself out if you really like batting? I have seen him score centuries that are faultless but the best innings by a mile was in a Sheffield Shield match against Victoria. Mark showed a determination not many people believe he possessed when he repelled Shane Warne and Merv Hughes to save a game which was all but lost. The pitch was turning a mile and Warne was in top form

109

landing the flipper and everything else that came out of his hand. I think Mark likes to get fired up when people doubt his determination and it gives him a special thrill facing the best bowlers. Mark says his best dig was in South Africa last year in the Third Test. It must have been something extra special to out rate this one at the SCG.

NUMBER FIVE

Richie Richardson

This may seem to be the most surprising selection considering Richie has retired from Test cricket. Out of sight is not out of mind and his attacking qualities would blend perfectly in my team. He was not all that flash against spinners but his characteristic cover drives were only surpassed by his swift despatch of any ball around middle and leg to the mid-wicket boundary. A fearsome hooker also meant that bowling short was not much use either. His fielding was superb and he was an inspirational leader.

NUMBER SIX

Steven Waugh

The player loved by crowds and loathed by the opposition, Steve is never one to bow to pressure or verbal abuse. His determination to guard his wicket makes him the most prized dismissal of any batsmen in the world. His footwork may be a little unorthodox but he has adapted it to suit himself and no-one else. He continues to score unbeaten centuries and is a master at batting with the lower order. Had he remained injury-free and able to keep bowling he would have developed into a world class all-rounder but this was not to be.

WICKET KEEPER

Ian Healy

There are many classy keepers in world cricket but none stand up to Ian's record. His keeping to Shane Warne over the years has proven he is world class. His role as a team motivator and handy batting make him the ideal choice to have in the trenches.

OPENING BOWLER

Wasim Akram

Wasim has it all, being able to swing a new ball both ways and seam or reverse swing the older one. His length and line are impeccable but his most lethal weapon is the chance of pace. Many a batsmen have lost their middle stump to this surprise ball. Wasim's action is one that some youngsters should model themselves on with a short run up and whippy front on delivery stride. He also gets through his overs quickly so batsmen do not have much time to think between balls.

OPENING BOWLER

Alan Donald

'White Lightning' as he has become known, has fearsome pace with a line around off-stump that makes it difficult to know which deliveries you can let go. He is the backbone of South Africa's attack and can sniff out a batting weakness in next to no time. Not a great swinger of the ball but not many bowlers could be at his pace. Also a great bowler with the old ball and will bowl until he drops.

FIRST CHANGE BOWLER

Curtly Ambrose

This may seem another strange selection but to obtain the right balance, Curtly must take the older ball even though he has been a great bowler against the opening batsmen with the new ball. I think he could play a more important role against the middle order after Akram and Donald have removed the openers. Curtly does not have the constant pace he used to employ but his change up in pace and ability to rear off a good length is still there. A fearsome sight to any batsman with a loping run to the wicket and line angled in at the body.

SPINNER

Shane Warne

His record speaks for itself. When Shane is spinning out of the rough on day four or five he is unplayable either for right or left-handers. He may have lost his flipper which was deadly early in his career but it's no use bowling it if it is not landing properly. I think he may have lost the confidence to bowl it now but when you have such a variety of leg-spinners and top-spinners in your bag, why bowl something less deadly. Has been on the operating table a few times for his shoulder injury but time away from the field will be the only thing stopping him from taking over 400 Test wickets.

SPINNER

Mushtaq Ahmed

Two leg-spinners may not be everyone's ideal attack but Mushtaq is by far the next best spinner available. On his day he may even be better than Warne and his wrong-un certainly is harder to pick than Shane's. His stock leg-spinner does not turn as far as Warne's but his variety is better disguised. Mushtaq continues to make world class batsmen look ordinary on all types of pitches.

CAPTAIN

Richie Richardson

The choice of a captain is not easy and it must be said that with this team virtually anyone should be able to act as skipper. I have eventually gone for Richie Richardson as he struck me as being a good communicator and an inspiration to his team. As the West Indies are not a combined nation except when cricket is mentioned I feel he has the right credentials to captain a world team.

Picking a twelfth man from this talent would be impossible but as the team has no genuine all-rounder then one of the bowlers must miss out. I would like to reserve the right to have a look at the pitch on match morning to decide whether a spinner or a fast bowler would carry the drinks.

Maybe we can change the laws to allow a twelve-man team in the future. This would make a batsman's job a little harder but that may be good for the game anyway. Australia has experimented with twelve players in the local One Day competition whereby only eleven players are allowed to bat or field but fieldsmen can be rotated at anytime. Food for thought for the law makers.

So, there are my selections. When you look at the calibre of players I have omitted like Mark Taylor, Mohammed Azzharudin, Hansie Cronje, Waqar Younis, Courtney Walsh and Angus Fraser, it was a difficult task. Not as difficult as it would be to play against them but I would put my hand up to umpire these men anytime, any place and I would pay money to do it.

CHAPTER SEVEN

COMMONSENSE UMPIRING: MY VIEWS ON SOME LAWS

The laws of cricket, most administrators will tell you, have stood the test of time. After all, very little has changed in the principle intentions of the laws since the first written copy dated 1744. Old stagers will say the game between bat and ball is traditional and to tamper with the laws is a recipe for disaster.

In true fact, the game has not kept pace with a fast-changing world and we are only kidding ourselves if we all agree that tradition must be maintained and changes not be made. International Cricket Council amendments made to cricket regulations, as opposed to actual law changes which have been implemented over the past decade have indeed been the most radical the game has experienced.

During this decade we have seen laws and regulations introduced to combat intimidatory fast bowling, ball tampering, fitness of light for play and the use of helmets. Cricket has seen the need to insist on minimum quotas of overs per day to ensure the paying public get value for their dollars. Heaven forbid, amendments have even been made to ensure bowlers cannot get away with illegal deliveries deemed as chucking, by implementing a 'three infringements and you are off' law.

The One Day game has been acknowledged as an extremely important part of the entertainment package and a different set of laws now covers fielding and bowling restrictions and a standard measurement for boundary lines and fences.

All of these changes are commendable and many were overdue. However, if we are to keep up with competing sports, I feel that some more radical alterations need to be made to how we play and present the game.

One of the most ridiculous laws is the allowance of leg byes. That extra runs should be allowed when a batsman is unable or incapable of making contact with the bat is to my mind ludicrous. I always thought that gear such as thigh pads were worn for protection not as a means of scoring runs.

Another reason to delete the law is because some modern batsman have become masters of deception by making it look like they are actually playing at the ball when in fact they are not. (One of the requirements in allowing runs is for the umpire to decide if a genuine attempt was made to actually play a stroke at the ball.) It is difficult for umpires to be required to make a judgement on whether a batsman's intentions are fair. Removing leg byes would allow us to concentrate on more important matters.

This is not a recent thought of mine either. Many years ago I took a Canadian visitor to the Sydney Cricket Ground to watch a One Day International. On the way to the ground I explained the basics of the game and as he was an avid base-ball fan, the concept of a different bat and ball game excited him.

The second ball of the game made contact with Geoff Marsh's thigh pad and careered down to the fine leg boundary. On explaining to my friend the reason for giving the batting team four extra runs he said it should not be allowed if the batsman was not capable of hitting the ball with his bat. A pretty fair comment. From that day, I have always believed that the leg bye law is out of place in the modern game and should be deleted. The only concession I would make is to allow the runs only if the batsman is trying to avoid being hit by a fast delivery above waist height.

The substitute fieldsman law provides an open invitation to use and abuse the provision. Recent ICC amendments have removed a lot of the abuse but from my experience the law is still open to improvements. The onus for deciding whether to allow a substitute falls upon the umpires. We are must be satis-fied that an injury or illness is genuine, yet I don't think there are very many of us who are qualified medical practitioners.

When we are confronted by team doctors and physio-therapists talking medical jargon about one type of injury or another, how are we to justify refusal of a replacement fieldsman? It is also amazing how a player can be at death's door late on a hot and humid day, leave the field for half an hour and return refreshed enough to take the new ball. Opening batsmen also become afflicted with a multitude of illness when they are in the field but are never too ill to open the batting when their turn comes.

These are some of the reasons why cricket should move forward and allow unconditional rotation of fieldsmen. A similar situation was tried in the recent domestic One Day Competition in Australia and I believe it worked very well. Teams were selected with twelve players but only eleven of the twelve are able to bat and this fact must be nominated prior to the toss. Unlimited interchange of fieldsmen was allowed and I found it worked very well with umpires not needing to be advised of some trumped up excuse to leave the field.

The LBW law is always contentious because it is the only law which requires an umpire to make a judgement on what he thinks will happen. We cop enough flak either way we go and there is one change which I would advocate to this law.

Presently, if a batsman makes contact on the ball with his bat prior to hitting the pads, he cannot be given out LBW. I ask the question—if the deflection off the bat was not enough to make the ball miss the stumps, then why should the batsman benefit? Along the same lines of the leg bye reasoning, I believe the batsman should be able to be given out under these circumstances. He has made an error of judgement or the bowling was a bit too good for him but yet, as the law states now, he survives. The law should be changed so that he can be given out.

I have a couple of suggested changes which will favour bowlers so to even things up there needs to be a change to help the batsman. The problems of the no ball law on foot placements have been talked about for about twenty years.

Changes that have been suggested like reverting to the back foot rule are not ones which I would favour.

Over the years, bowlers have been getting fitter and

faster. This has been countered somewhat by batsmen wearing helmets, high tech thigh guards and vastly improved protective gloves. Some even have chest protectors as thick as telephone books. Fieldsmen are able to crowd the batsmen and feel safe wearing helmets and shin protectors.

The length of the pitch which is 22 yards has not changed in two hundred years and that may have been all right when the bowlers were slower and unable to bowl fast all day as the likes of Ambrose, Donald, Walsh and McGrath do these days. (Although the batsmen facing Larwood and Voce may have disagreed.) Twenty two yards seems a long way until a bowler oversteps by a foot and sends the ball searing up around your throat.

The fast bowling of today is something the law makers could not have originally imagined and there is a need to keep the bowlers back behind the line. My proposal would be to not allow the bowler to make any contact with the front line at all. Therefore he would have to ensure his front foot landed some twelve inches (depending on the size of his foot) further back than at present.

This may not sound like much of a change but I am sure most batsmen would appreciate the extra reaction time for a legal delivery and heaven knows they may even benefit by an earlier call of no ball and get a chance of a free swing. It rarely happens now.

Finally, to ensure the bowlers take things seriously, I would like to see the penalty imposed for bowling a no ball rise from one run to ten runs. This type of penalty should have the desired effect and captains would not be happy if their bowlers continually over stepped the line. No balls are not good for the game and are there for good reason similar to the foot fault rule in tennis. Apart from keeping a fast bowler at a fair distance from the batsman, no balls just become boring as Richie Benaud quite often states on television.

So there you have my suggestions for improving the game. Would these changes be for the better and keep up with the modern world? We may never know unless the law makers give these suggestions a chance.

CHAPTER EIGHT

THE WEST INDIES
AND AUSTRALIA
DAY BLUES

Test match umpiring has its ups and downs. It also has the capability to be mentally exhausting and it is every umpire's nightmare that a match will go right down to the wire and a decision is going to make the difference between a marginal win or loss. Every umpire I have spoken to would always have a preference for one team to win by a large margin—it eases the pressure. Long and tedious draws are next on the scale when it appears likely the game win fizzle out to a tame draw. The nightmare of a close finish came true for me on Australia Day 1993.

The West Indies were still the dominant force in world cricket when Brian Lara came of age in Sydney, scoring his maiden Test century and making it a memorable one by finishing on 277. Had there not been a misunderstanding with Carl Hooper resulting in him being run out, he may have finished with 500! The Aussies must have been grateful as he had been dropped by Steve Waugh in the gully when only on 117. Greg Matthews was also convinced he had him plumb leg before wicket on 196 but I kept my finger in my pocket.

The Sydney Test finished in a draw and Australia went to Adelaide with a one nil lead in the series with two more to he played. Despite only having a one game advantage, Australia had been on top for the majority of the series played except for that Sydney Test. The Adelaide game was to be a low scoring affair which was unusual as the Adelaide Oval pitch is generally regarded as the best batting strip in Australia, if not the world.

The match appeared to turn in favour of Australia when the Windies collapsed in the second innings with Tim May taking a career best of 5 wickets for 9 runs. This left 186 runs to win which should have been a fairly easy target for any team to chase. Unless, of course, you are playing the West Indies. A bowling attack featuring Courtney Walsh and Curtly Ambrose will always back themselves to bowl a team out, but even they must have had reservations on a pitch which was still playing quite well. There had been a break for rain on the third afternoon and overcast conditions on day four ensured the pitch would not be as dry as originally predicted and it held together better than expected.

Players are under enormous pressure to perform on the final day of a Test and even though this was only the fourth day, a lot had happened with over 30 wickets falling so far. Such situations are no place for the weak of heart or body. Pressure manifests itself in many different ways and some of the shot selection was, by Test standards, pretty ordinary.

With the game in the balance, I remember the first ball

after the lunch break which Steven Waugh managed to spoon straight to Keith Arthurton at cover who almost dropped the simplest of catches. Had he done so Australia would have been only 3 for 80 instead of 4 wickets down. I blame both of those players for the predicament in which I eventually found myself.

It was a poor delivery played even more poorly by Waugh and was almost dropped in eager fashion by Arthurton. If Steven had the shot to play over again I am certain he would have chosen differently—I for one certainly wished he had! But that is the joy and uncertainty of the game and the results that pressure situations bring.

A steady fall of wickets saw Border, Healy, Warne and Hughes depart. When McDermott joined May the score was 9 for 142 and with another 46 runs to make the chance of an Australian win looked forlorn. The Windies were gearing up to celebrate but the strangest things happen in cricket matches. The scoring edged along through ones and twos and sensible batting saw the total reach 170.

That was when the game changed complexion. Tension rose to unbearable levels with the realisation that a miss hit could decide the result either way. I was in unknown territory. There can be no training that will ever prepare you perfectly for this type of situation.

It is quite all right to say 'stay calm, don't panic' but when everyone around you starts to show signs of the strain, you are only one step from heart failure. I said to myself, 'If Richardson and Walsh are showing the pressure, what hope do I have'?

Between deliveries the West Indies were all chat, but as

the bowler began his run up you could hear a pin drop. The batsmen suffered too. At times I thought a single could be turned into two but May and McDermott were cautious knowing that a silly run out would cost Australia the match. So the long crawl towards victory continued.

If you asked each player now, they would all say they were cool but I can assure you they were not. My partner Len King and I reached peak concentration and Len was a great support. I think we made eye contact after every ball in that final hour or so. To make a simple mistake then was to court disaster.

Things race through your mind. What if I allow a 7 ball over and something happens off that delivery? What if I miss an obvious no ball and a wicket falls? What about a short run? How many bouncers has he bowled now? All of these decisions involve elementary umpiring skills which come naturally when necessary. Yet now these questions filled my mind and were oppressive and insistent.

I recall having a conversation with both May and McDermott at various stages whilst they were at my end but I could not remember a word that was said. It was small talk designed to ease their nerves—but what about mine? When the first ball of what turned out to be the last over was bowled by Walsh with two runs needed to win, I chatted quietly to Courtney on his way back. I told him that he was creeping up with his front foot. I didn't want to be calling a no ball now which would even the scores, however had he gone over the line I would have done so. That was the level of my concentration. I'll bet Courtney would not remember the conversation.

That last ball will be forever in my memory and obviously in many thousands of others as well. It was banged in short and rose around shoulder height. McDermott's bat and gloves rose with the ball and just as it went past him he flinched and turned his head. I was certain the ball made contact with his glove and the sound confirmed it. To no-one's surprise there was an appeal when the ball was caught and I had no hesitation in deciding to give McDermott out.

The trouble was that my right hand would not move and I froze momentarily. Eventually the finger went up after what seemed like an eternity. After seeing it on replay, the delay in giving him out was no longer than I normally take. It just seemed like an eternity. The realisation that the game was over also took a few seconds to register.

When Len and I walked off I could feel my knees trembling and I would have actually preferred to be carried off on a stretcher. Just thinking about it again makes my stomach churn and my legs feel like rubber. Allan Border, despite his disappointment, came in to the umpires' room to thank us which is a rarity for Allan. He was never big on compliments towards umpires and although I was surprised, I genuinely appreciated his gesture.

It was not until a few days later that the decision was analysed. The slow motion footage from behind the wicket keeper showed that the ball may have hit McDermott on the peak of the helmet and I have to concede that it looks to have done so. The facts were that I had based my decision on a completely different perspective.

I had decided that the ball hit him on the glove as he was trying to manoeuvre his bat and hands out of the way and the television footage from my end does not confirm or deny that possibility. I was still certain that I had been right until McDermott publicly stated that he did not hit the ball. That was a strange statement as it came from an article by the same journalist who reported McDermott's feelings the day after the game. It was in this article that McDermott had admitted the ball brushed the glove.

Be that as it may, the decision at the time was out and no-one can alter that. It just goes to prove that all we have to do to get things right is to sit up with the reverse angle camera or have the right to change our decision a week after the game when a player decides he didn't think he was out. If only umpiring could be that easy.

An interesting follow up to the decision came when I was umpiring the South Africa versus Australia Test again at the Adelaide Oval exactly twelve months later. McDermott was batting with Ian Healy when he fended at a short rising delivery from Brian McMillan. It was not dissimilar to the shot McDermott had offered to the Walsh delivery. After the ball had passed, Healy said to Craig, 'Practise that again, only this time drop you hands as it passes'. The three of us smiled at the irony.

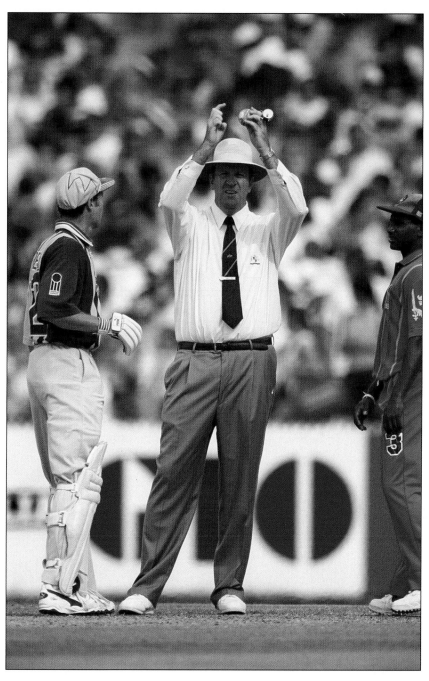

Darrell Hair calling for a new ball in the One Day Final, Australia v Sri Lanka, MCG, January 1996. (*Australian Picture Library*)

Peter Parker explaining to Ranatunga that cricket balls do not normally have these funny scratches on them. Sri Lanka was later cleared of any wrong doing in the ball tampering incident.

Enjoying a quiet moment with Dickie Bird in Hobart.

Steve Bucknor is acknowledged as one of the best in the world. Here he has completed his morning ritual of the pitch inspection at the MCG. I have been honoured to stand with Steve in three matches.

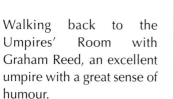

Walking back to the Umpires' Room with Graham Reed, an excellent umpire with a great sense of humour.

South Africa and Australia meet at the MCG. This game was marred by rain.

Umpiring some 'Kwik Cricket' in London. It was a pleasure to assist the ICC at one of the East End schools. Most of the kids come from poor backgrounds but really live for their cricket.

The headmistress from one of the East End schools getting some pointers from a couple of experts.

In the company of fellow cheats! This was a rare opportunity to gather some knowledge. Left to right are David French, David Shepherd, Ted Wykes, Darrell Hair and Tom Brooks.

One of the pleasures of being on the road. Barry Jarman (Jar) and Henry Blofield (Blowers) are great company and appreciate a good red.

Young Darrell (back row, fourth from left) representing New South Schoolboys under 14 years. Other notables are Ian Davis (front row, first on right) and manager, Stan Gilchrist (standing, left). The selectors did a good job with this team as every player went on to first grade or higher.

THE WEST INDIES AND AUSTRALIA DAY BLUES

During the late seventies and early eighties I was still playing club cricket for Mosman. The West Indies were awesome and undisputed champions in both forms of the game. Clive Lloyd had an endless supply of extremely mean fast bowlers and he marshalled this artillery with ruthless disregard for opposing teams. Even on the odd occasion when his batsman failed, Clive was still able to unleash his bowlers and win the game.

Things have changed in the late nineties. The West Indies are no longer feared and the endless supply of fast bowling terrors seems to have dried up. So too have the dashing batsmen. There is only one name feared now, Brian Lara. The sheer natural talent of Lara makes for exciting stroke play and sometimes it just goes on and on and on!

Brian took a while to score his maiden Test century but when he did, he made it a big one. His 277 on the SCG in January 1993 was pure class and I was lucky enough to be in the middle of things again. He was dropped by Steve Waugh when on 117 and most times you think it won't cost you many extra runs. Greg Matthews was also convinced he had Lara LBW on 196 and Greg has never forgiven me for shaking my head that day. In fact Lara could have possibly broken the world record that day on a perfect Sydney pitch but was run out in a mix up with Carl Hooper.

It is not very often that you become part of a world record. Not many people will ever remember that I was on the ground when Lara smashed his record 375 runs in Antigua and quite rightly, no-one should really care. The fact that I was there to witness the innings means a lot to me though. Apart from my sentimentality about the occasion, he did bat exceptionally well and it is interesting to compare the innings with other members of the 300 Club in Test cricket.

Lara scored 10 more runs and batted for 152 more minutes than did Gary Sobers 36 years before when Sobers scored 365. Lara batted 31 minutes less that Len Hutton did at The Oval fifty-six years earlier when Hutton made 364. Sobers and Hutton were both part of winning teams whereas Lara's side could only draw with England. Indeed, history shows us the result is usually a drawn match when someone makes a triple century as only four games have resulted in a win to the team with the triple centurion. The other nine instances have resulted in a draw. Even the great Sir Don Bradman could not help his team to a win when he scored his two triple centuries. So Lara is in elite company, isn't he?

Records are made to be broken but it would appear that scoring a mountain of runs in one innings does not help your team to win a cricket match. Still Lara's innings in itself was a gem and Brian did not give a chance. One ball from Andy Caddick did pass at catchable height through third slip but he was around 250 at the time so Atherton had long dispensed with an attacking field. Caddick even enquired if I thought it was a 'genuine' edge—in other words did he actually get the ball to do something to fool Lara. I had to inform a crestfallen Caddick that I most certainly did not think so as he trudged off back down to third man.

The pitch invasion which followed Lara's achievement was something else again. In Australia, we are lucky to have tight security at all grounds which apart from the odd drunk streaker gaining access, there are no disruptions of this nature. On the third morning with Lara on about 325 the umpires were asked by the ground security if they had any objections to Sir Garfield Sobers entering the ground together with a television crew to record the anticipated world record. Sir Garfield was to shake Lara's hand in a brief ceremony.

I had no problems with that but I did enquire as to whether the security at the ground could cope with a possible invasion by the fans. I was assured that steps had been taken to ensure such a thing could not happen. Unfortunately, a dozen or so policemen were never going to be able to cope with any crowd disturbance so it was with some misgivings that I noticed that 'reinforcements' had not arrived as Brian edged close to the world record.

Something in the back of my mind also warned me that there may be a riot if he did not break the record. There is nothing like the thought of returning home in a wooden box to spur on the concentration levels. I did not want to have had to give him out so I was more relieved than Brian when he despatched a short one from Chris Lewis to the mid-wicket boundary to surpass the record. I still do not know if the ball actually did make it to the fence as it disappeared into a sea of fans rushing towards the centre. I signalled four runs anyway. These fans were joined by the very same policemen who were supposed to be keeping them off together with ground staff, gate stewards and for all I know, the ladies running the after-noon tea stalls!

Brian was mobbed by thousands of unruly spectators and I have no idea if Sir Garfield made it out there either. I am reliably informed that he did, it was just impossible to see if he did. During the disturbance, I stood between the two tallest men on the ground, Chris Lewis and Andy Caddick and as a result, I felt quite safe. Michael Atherton saw spectators jumping up and down on the pitch and requested that I may wish to get them off. My reply cannot be repeated here but rest assured I did not entertain any thoughts of intervening, and suggested to Michael that he might like to remove them himself.

Order was finally restored some fifteen minutes later and the ground was cleared and ready for resumption of play. To my complete amazement the stumps and bails had remained in tact at both ends and no-one had souvenired the ball which was located out near the mid wicket boundary. At least I was assured by England that it was the same ball. If this had happened in Australia I am sure we would have needed to find new stumps and another ball. Probably says something about our convict past.

I am also reliably informed that Brian came perilously close to treading on his stumps when he played that pull shot. That would have been Steve Bucknor's responsibility and possibly a life-threatening decision.

Brian Lara is a world champion batsman and coming with the tag is a certain manner which does not endear him to Australian cricketers. They feel he is a troublemaker but I say it is a mark of respect if the Australians really do feel that way about him. Australia's best players fear no-one these days and if someone like Lara gains their attention in this way, it means they are concerned and see him as a threat.

I have never experienced any dramas with Brian not accepting decisions—he always accepts them on the field with good grace and it is something that a lot of other players should take note of. The only safe place to let off steam is in the dressing room and Brian followed that principle after being given out caught behind by Ian Healy in the Sydney Test in January 1997. David Shepherd was uncertain if the ball had carried to Healy and sought my opinion. I confirmed that it had and Brian departed quickly. It was unfortunate however that he chose to visit the Australian dressing room even before he had taken off his pads to indicate his displeasure at Ian Healy. I am still at a loss to understand why he took this strange decision as the press quickly found out and it made Brian look a little foolish. I wonder what the members in the SCG bar thought at the sight. Maybe they thought he had forgotten where his own dressing room was.

The only other time I had the possibility of a flare up with Brian was in Perth at the end of the series. The West Indies had already lost the series but were on top in the Fifth Test and heading for a face saving win. A lot had been said and a large number of players had been 'chatting' each other which is, and always has been impossible for umpires to hear, so I was surprised when Lara indicated that if the Australians did not shut up he was going to ram his bat down a couple of their throats.

He was acting as a runner for the injured skipper Courtney Walsh at the time so it was obvious he had heard a few uncomplimentary remarks and lost his cool. The fact that Walsh had Lara out there acting as a runner was an unnecessary irritation anyway. A number of other batsmen were capable of doing the job. Carl Hooper, for example, is the fastest man between wickets in Test cricket—why couldn't Walsh have him sent out to do the running? We all agree that there is nothing in the laws to say who may or may not act as a runner.

The other umpire, Peter Willey and myself decided that it may be better to prevent any bloodshed. We called a mid-pitch conference with Taylor and Walsh to sort things out.

Various views were aired by both captains as to what should be acceptable behaviour and agreement was reached to cease hostilities and therefore bloodshed was averted. I would rather not have to be involved in such conversations but I had visions of Javed Miandad attempting to bash Dennis Lillee with his bat on the same ground many years ago. Mind you, that was after Dennis had connected with a well aimed boot on Miandad's backside. I only saw that one on television but now I was right in the middle of a potentially much worse situation. Something controversial always seems to be happen in Perth. It must be either the heat, the cracks in the pitch or just the fresh air from the 'Fremantle Doctor' that causes the full moon effect over there.

The aftermath of the incident was further inflamed when Lara decided to go public with his views on the attitude and behaviour of the Australians. During a press conference he left little doubt that he felt the Australians were rude, crude and abusive and had treated Robert Samuels, the West Indies opening batsman with scant respect.

I always thought you had to prove yourself and earn respect from the opposition and the fact that Samuels made some runs did not necessarily mean the Aussies had changed their opinion of his talent. Lara also indicated that Australia were always the instigators and never the victims but anyone who believes that statement is living in a fairyland. The West Indies give as much and mostly more than they take.

Mark Taylor did weigh in with his comments under a

headline in the *West Australian* newspaper on 4 February straight after losing by 10 wickets inside three days.

LARA TO BLAME FOR BAD BLOOD

Not such a good headline that could have been construed as sour grapes. Taylor was critical of Lara's on field demeanour and said there was no doubt that Lara was an antagonist. Taylor went on to say that he had great respect for Lara's ability but felt he paid too much attention to the way the Aussies had treated Robert Samuels. The whole episode did not give the heir apparent much credibility. But then again if one player goes through the press to make a point, then others must certainly be allowed to follow suit.

The other disappointing aspect of this match was the performance of Curtly Ambrose, not from his bowling ability but from a display of petulance which was neither warranted or becoming of a player of his international standard. During the Australian second innings in which they were bowled out very cheaply, Ambrose began bowling a succession of no balls. After I made three calls for overstepping, Ambrose changed to around the wicket and continued to infringe with not only his front foot but also his back foot which was landing wide of the return crease.

The batsmen at the time were Shane Warne and Andy Bichel and there was more than a hint of attempted intimid-ation in the way Ambrose was bowling. Both Bichel and Warne had taken blows to the body and I informed Courtney Walsh that should Ambrose continue bowling in this manner,

I would have no hesitation in warning and no balling him for intimidation. This would have been a silly way for Ambrose to end his final match in Australia and finally sanity prevailed and the over was completed. A 15 ball over in Test cricket is probably not a record but nine no balls may just about creep in with a chance. Unfortunately I remember the crowd booing Ambrose when he finally completed the over. Everything considered it was not the way that Australian fans should remember a man who is one of the all time greats of fast bowling.

Brian has recently taken over the captaincy from Courtney Walsh and he has an unenviable task before him. Walsh and Ambrose are on the verge of retirement and to date, no-one has stepped up with authority to take their place. The batting has a steady feel about it but a desperate search is under way to find a dominant opening pair to replace Haynes and Greenidge.

The middle order batting has a steady feel about it and apart from Lara as the stroke maker, Chanderpaul and Adams are more collectors of runs. The form of Carl Hooper has never been consistent enough to rank him as a true world class player despite his magnificent style and fitness level. If anyone is to make a success of captaining his national team Lara must be the one most capable. He has self assurance and can lead from the front which is expected of Test match captains these days.

I have completed two tours to the West Indies and in all the eight of my twenty-six Test matches have involved them. During that time it is reasonable to say that they are not the force they were in the late eighties. Teams no longer fear them especially the Australians, and so far there has been little indication of a replacement pace attack coming to the fore. This may be the case for some years to come.

I don't believe they are finished however, as world cricket is now a much tougher place in which to compete. The gap between nations has narrowed and it is more and more difficult to win Tests. Who really knows, the new Ambrose, Walsh and Haynes may just be a match or two away.

One huge problem facing cricket in the West Indies is the constant battle to produce pitches suitable for Test match cricket. This led to the unfortunate abandonment of the First Test of the series against England at Jamaica in February 1998. Much has since been said and written about the decision by the umpires, Steve Bucknor and Venkat, to abandon the game after just 12 overs had been bowled. There were even suggestions that the match referee Barry Jarman had taken the decision himself. This was absolute rubbish of course as the umpires are the only people empowered to take such a decision.

There was also the suggestion that had the West Indies been batting, the match would have continued at their insistence. I have only seen video footage of the England innings and it was certainly frightening viewing. There is no doubt in my view that the pitch was unsuitable for first class cricket however the reasons for the presentation of such a pitch remain a mystery. Only three weeks later Jimmy Adams scored a double century on the same ground in the President's Cup competition and as that game finished in a draw it suggests there is not a long term problem with the playing surface.

The next Test was to be in Trinidad and it was one which I followed in the news with keen interest back in Australia as I was appointed to the following Test also to be played at Queens Park, Trinidad. Stories of another under-prepared pitch were not the news I really wanted to hear and a low scoring game saw the West Indies win by three wickets with Carl Hooper and David Williams combining make the winning runs after England looked likely to snatch a win.

My Test produced another result, this time a win to England by three wickets with my old friend Angus Fraser collecting another ten wicket haul which ensured him of a well earned 'man of the match' award. The pitch was an interesting one which kept considerably low on the first three days. This resulted in quite a few LBW decisions and suggestions that this pitch was not up to Test match standard. In fact the pitch played much better on the fourth and fifth days which is quite the opposite to what should occur. Overall, it probably was not what you would call a Test match pitch but it certainly was not dangerous like the one at Sabina Park.

After Trinidad, I had a few days off before heading to Guyana for the Fourth Test. What confronted us there was a dry and dusty pitch which did not look like being up to Test match standard. Quite often the toss decides the final result and that was certainly the case for this Test. The West Indies won the toss and batted first scoring over 350. With the pitch gradually crumbling, England had virtually no chance and although a last wicket stand avoided the follow on, England lost in four days.

Many fond memories will remain with me about West Indies cricket. My first One Day International involved them and Richie Richardson, realising it was my first in the big time, made a point of congratulating me and wishing me well before the game started. It was the one and only time that a captain has done this and it was a moment to cherish. This gesture was typical of Richie who was one of those special people you meet as an umpire along the way. The wonderful batting of Lara and bowling of Ambrose and Walsh always remind me of how lucky I have been to be able to observe them at such close quarters.

Once you get used to the heat, both on and off the field, the Caribbean is a wonderful place to umpire cricket and meet the greats of yesteryear, who always turn up to watch Test matches. One very special time, however, was my most recent trip when I was blessed with the company of ICC referee Barry Jarman and former West Indian umpire, Clyde Cumberbatch.

Clyde and Barry have beautiful singing voices and at various times would burst into song for no particular reason. After dining out one night in Trinidad, their rendition of 'Ole Man River' just seemed to make all the hard work worth-while. Cool ale, warm night air and the serenading voices made me realise how worthwhile a career in umpiring can be.

Another factor to come out of Guyana was the age-old argument about what constitutes a genuine attempt to play at the ball. Players seem to have been coached to tuck the bat well behind the pad when playing spinners. This quite often lessens the possibility of a bat pad catch. The style is usually adopted by players limited in their ability to play good spin bowling. It may also be utilised when a batsman is trying to frustrate a bowler with the hope that he will then bowl something loose.

This style of defence is not the umpire's problem until such time as a decision whether to allow leg byes arises or the bowler shouts for a leg before wicket decision. The law is quite clear that a batsman may be given out should the umpire be of the opinion that the ball is going to hit the stumps even though the ball may impact outside the line of the off stump.

Jimmy Adams chose to play to the spin of Tufnell and Croft in this manner during the Test and I gave him out twice for doing so. Ambrose also went the same way in the second innings. I managed to cop some flak for making these decisions (what else is new?) but I stand by them 100 per cent.

When it becomes clear to me that the pad is being used to defend, then a batsman is in peril if he is hit outside the off-stump with the ball spinning in. I even feel that some umpires duck their responsibility by giving the benefit of the doubt to the batsman.

How many times do we see batsmen confused by tanta-lising flight or unable to deal with vicious spin who simply kick the ball away and get away with it? Is it the bowler's fault that a batsman is baffled by the subtle disguise of those who spin the ball both ways? My view is that this type of play may be the reason that so few good finger spinners are operating in international cricket. They are often deprived of taking wickets as a result of this type of pad play.

I earned the nickname 'Hair Trigger' in the press in the West Indies, and people such as the knowledgeable writer and commentator, Tony Cozier wrote that I had taken up a vendetta against this style of pad play. He even went so far as to say I had no right to make such judgements on Test cricketers. The implication was that their careers are put at risk with my style of umpiring. This, in my opinion, is utter rubbish. A bowler's career is also at stake if he does not take wickets. Providing a bowler is bowling fairly, I see no reason why I should ignore a very important aspect of the laws.

Cricket should always be a game between bat and ball, not pad and ball. I agree that giving four batsmen out in a Test match, (Hooper was the other one) is unusual, but if the same set of circumstances were to occur again when I am umpiring I would make the same decisions.

A look at some of the statistics from Tests and first class matches in Australia over the past four years will show that quite a few batsmen have been given out in this way by umpires other than myself. I say we are doing our job properly and well by invoking laws which have been ignored too often and for far too long in the past.

CHAPTER NINE

THE ONE DAY GAME AND THE FUTURE OF CRICKET

Cricket in Australia has many competitors. Football codes are encroaching more than ever on the traditional summer season. Basketball and baseball have been the success stories of the nineties with slick marketing schemes and American-style hype. They also have the benefits of being a convenient sport either played indoors without weather problems or, as in baseball's case, the time factor of being played over a shorter period appeals to families.

Summer in Australia has many other distractions. The generally staid nature of first class cricket does not have the same appeal as it may have in years gone by. There is also the time factor as matches can last several hours and weather problems with rain or bad light can compound the problems of keeping people keen and interested in cricket. One Day Cricket has been put forward as the saviour of the game. There is still a division among cricket followers about the proper place for the one day game. Some will tell you they would rather cut their throat than watch one day cricket. I have yet to know anyone who took such a drastic step!

Is the one day game all that different from what we know as 'The Real Cricket'? I do not believe it is when you consider that most club and social cricket is in fact played over one day with either restrictions on time or the number of overs. There is also the small matter of funding. Let's face it, programming is easier if you know when a game is going to start or finish and whether we like it or not we cannot afford to be without the revenue that televised one day cricket provides.

One day limited overs cricket became a winner during the World Series Cricket days. Spectators were not attending the longer form of the game and few had the time available to sit for five days in front of a television set. World Series Cricket changed the way the game was marketed. The advent of night cricket made it easier for families to watch a game and the fact that there would be a winner declared that same day.

I believe that one day cricket revived interest to such an extent that we now have sellout days for Test matches. Fans have been introduced to seeing their heroes performing under lights and under pressure. Those same people are now extending their interest to Test matches. The general skills of cricketers have improved, in particular the fitness and fielding

The umpire's role in the one day form has also changed. We are required to be more involved in rulings to keep the game moving and interesting. Wides, no balls, fielding and bowling restrictions are all aspects requiring action by umpires which keep us in the limelight. The non-stop action also requires us to be under pressure for longer periods. Three and a half hour sessions of scampering batsmen and hustling fieldsmen are not conducive to catching up on rest.

Television assistance for run out, stumping, catches and boundary decisions has made our job a little easier but the trade off is that more scrutiny is now on our other decisions such as LBW and bat/pad catches.

The bowlers are severely restricted with few attacking options. On the flatter pitches usually prepared for the run fast bowlers are told to deliver the ball constantly in the strike zone otherwise us umpires will usually call wides. If he bowls a bouncer we have to call no ball. The playing conditions say that the ball must not be bowled negatively and must give the batsman a reasonable opportunity to score runs.

However, I do believe that bowlers should be allowed to at least try something especially when a batsman is advancing down the pitch and I would change the conditions to allow one fast short-pitched ball per over. This is providing that the ball does not actually go over the batsman's head and such a move would allow a bowler some sort of surprise element. It may even entice a batsman to play a hook shot adding further excitement for the crowd.

The 'surprise' bouncer is still alive and well in present one day cricket and is usually produced in a one sided game where one team is winning quite easily.

Seeing a bouncer bowled at that stage is usually just a reminder to the batsman that he may be on top today but maybe not next week. I remember Steve Waugh bowling one to Curtly Ambrose at the Sydney Cricket Ground and the look on Curtly's face was of complete surprise but quickly changed to indicate it had gone in the little black book. I'm certain it has been repaid a few times over by now.

The second change that I would advocate is the complete disallowance of runs scored as leg byes. I have spoken about my feelings on this aspect at length in another chapter and I feel quite strongly that the game should be played between bat and ball. The pads, arm guards and chest protectors are only there to prevent injury. An abnormally large amount of runs are scored due to the infamous leg bye and sometimes up to 10 per cent of the total can be accrued in this fashion. It is sometimes impossible for the fielding captain to cut off these runs with fielding restrictions only allowing certain options in the field. An experiment in dispensing with leg byes would be worthwhile.

The real future and survival of cricket relies on the development and introduction of new nations to One Day International status. To currently have ten nations with one day status is not enough for cricket to gather acceptance as a true global sport. Every four years the World Cup provides for emerging nations to be included and we have already witnessed Kenya defeating the West Indies.

In early 1997 I travelled to Malaysia to umpire in the ICC Trophy matches. This series decides who would play in the next World Cup in England. The three teams to qualify were Scotland, Kenya and Bangladesh with the latter taking out the final against Kenya. I was very impressed with the talent on show. Bangladesh is a fanatical cricketing nation but more importantly the talent produced by their coach, former West Indies opening batsman Gordon Greenidge, was of true international standard. Winning that tournament also promoted Bangladesh to full One Day International status putting them firmly on the path to their goal of becoming a Test playing nation.

Kenya had some outstanding players but playing on synthetic pitches did not suit their style. I think they would be more at home on turf and with a little bit more bounce and pace their batsmen and bowlers would be very competitive.

Batsmen Maurice Odumbe and Stephen Tikolo have already played first class cricket in South Africa and I would like to see more of fast bowler Martin Suji who was young and enthusiastic.

Scotland won the play off for third place and subsequently the final spot for World Cup positions with Ireland finishing fourth. Naturally exposure to the English first class scene, with several players from both sides gathering experience in county cricket, makes it easier for both these teams but development should not be curtailed just because of convenient location. Most cricket is spread around the globe with vast distances to be travelled—there is a lot to be done and one day cricket is playing its part in getting there.

Every trip overseas has had its high moments but the greatest sight of all in Malaysia was at the official closing dinner with the President of the Malaysian Cricket Association, Prince Tunku Imran, who proved he was a champion at karaoke. His rendition of 'Cotton Fields' had everyone in raptures and many even joined him on stage dancing to the beat. Not me, though, I have two left feet!

CHAPTER TEN

SLEDGING—NOTHING NEW UNDER THE SUN

*S*hould *any player or players conduct themselves in a disorderly manner whilst engaged in a match, the Association shall have the power to fine, suspend from further play or otherwise deal with such offenders as may be decided.* Extract from the rules governing electoral and club matches played under the management of the New South Wales Cricket Association during the season 1893–94.

Players and Team Officials must at all times accept the umpire's decision. Players must not show dissent at the umpire's decision. Players and Team Officials shall not at any time engage in conduct unbecoming to an international player or team official which could bring them or the game into disrepute. International Cricket Council Code of Conduct 1998.

Law 42: Unfair Play

1. Responsibility of Captains

The Captains are responsible at all times for ensuring that play is conducted within the spirit of the game as well as within the laws. MCC Official Laws of Cricket.

My first contact with the phenomenon which became known as sledging was very early in my playing days. This leads me to believe that this type of behaviour has always been a part of cricket except that today it creates all types of problems if not handled properly.

As a young boy of fifteen I recall playing in a men's district match at Molong near Orange. Our opening bowlers were having a devil of a time removing the opposition and were frustrated that none of them could seem to find the middle of their bats. Edges and miss hits were zooming to all parts of the ground. This frustration was amplified by the fact that it was about 95 degrees and the prospect of a cold beer seemed to be getting further and further away.

One of our bowlers, obviously feeling somewhat tired and thirsty, came up with an outburst which had everybody in stitches. 'If you use the edge once more, I'll be using your ribs for kettle drums'. When the laughter subsided, the rather sedate farmer holding the bat merely smiled and played another top edge over slips for four. What followed was a barrage of bouncers which Larwood and Jardine would have been delighted to see. A few bruises were inflicted from some fearsome blows to the body.

Shortly afterwards and feeling somewhat unsettled, the farmer found his middle stump uprooted from a perfectly delivered yorker. It was a case of winning the battle but not the war as our star fast bowler was now exhausted and retired to the shade of the fine leg boundary for the rest of the game. Needless to say we lost the game more through frustration than lack of ability.

I began playing when the game was an amateur pastime played for fun and enjoyment and have seen it grow to be a full-time professional sport where your performance or lack of it decides whether you have a job next week. The extra pressures may have taken a lot of the enjoyment out of playing but every major sport in the world has gone the same way.

This does not excuse poor behaviour or sportsmanship but we cannot ignore the pressures international players are put under either. Cricket matches are beamed live into millions of homes and children want to emulate their idols.

Most of the players direct a lot of energy into gaining the psychological advantage and no-one wants to deny them the opportunity of coming out on top even if it requires a bit of sledging. They have to live with their actions but the onus for keeping the game within the spirit of the laws rests fairly and squarely with the captains. Many captains in the past have abdicated their responsibilities in this regard but I am happy to say all leaders I have encountered keep a watchful eye on the hotheads.

There are match referees watching every move and who are only too willing to remove a percentage of a match fee should there be an indiscretion. Television cameras pick up even the most innocent of actions to help sensationalise the coverage. Quite often the image of what has been captured on television does not equate to the real story on the field.

Decisions such as an LBW given not out because the umpire decides the ball hit the edge of the bat first, even though it was going to uproot the middle stump is a classic example. Another may be a caught behind appeal when there was a noise caused by the bat hitting to pad or ground but no contact bat and ball.

The other problem we have is the way that television and radio commentators as well as newspaper reporters quite often tell a story to the public which is low on facts but high on controversy. I challenge all involved in the media to take part in a full examination on the laws so that when something does happen, it should not be sensationalised through lack of knowledge.

Another part of the problem of misinterpretation is that in most sports there is a specific signal given for each decision. Cricket is not like that and I am the first to admit that there are many grey areas such as the ones mentioned above, which are not immediately clear to all spectators. Indeed they are quite often not clear to the players on the field until they ask for and receive a clarification.

I am in favour of provision being made for umpires to give a clear and precise signal as to why a decision like say, LBW has been given not out. By making it clear you felt it was too high, missing leg stump or the batsman got an edge with his bat, a lot of irritation would be averted on the field. Even being wired for sound like the football referees would have advantages. It would also rid us of speculation about why a bowler has been spoken to at the end of an over for things such as getting close to the danger area and damaging the pitch.

We have long been told that decisions should not be

discussed with any player except the captain who has a right under the laws to seek an explanation. This attitude is changing and I believe it is for the better. I see no problem in giving an explanation to someone who seeks it in a civil manner. When a bowler asks you a question as he is walking back to his mark or at the end of an over, I have no drama with giving him an honest answer. Surely we owe it to the game to play our part in making it easier on all concerned.

After all, football codes such as Rugby League and Rugby Union have their referees wired for sound, both for communication between each other and letting the entire television audience know precisely why a penalty has or has not been given. We even hear players being cautioned for foul or offensive play. I wonder what some players would say if this were introduced for cricket! Even take it a step further and have these messages available to the people at the ground via the public address system—let us not just keep the television viewer updated.

Umpires come in all shapes, sizes and with many propensities. Some concentrate on the rules more than they concentrate on the human relations aspects of the game. We have to give the benefit of the doubt first in our decisions but there can be no place in the modern game to leave any one in doubt as to why we made the decision.

The umpire's role in clamping a lid on the aggression can go a long way towards keeping themselves and the players out of trouble. The umpire/player relationship sets the tone for a 'good day at the office' for everyone. Being a good umpire requires more than just having a pulse and a white hat. It not just a matter of who's right but what's right.

When you have the best players a nation can offer on the field it makes for a lot of tension and a lot of aggression. Mention names like Warne, the Waugh brothers, Cullinan, Cronje, Donald, Walsh, Ambrose and Lara and you realise that they are playing for keeps. Tempers will fray and a lot of verbal jousting is going to take place before a Test match is won or lost. They will take every advantage they can get and if there is a chink in the character it will more than likely be found out and worked on.

By and large it is pretty much ego stuff and I am most surprised if they lose their cool to the extent of becoming verbally abusive. There has only been one occasion where it has been necessary to call upon the captains to take control. This was the Test in Perth when Peter Willey and I had to intervene and have a long discussion with Taylor and Walsh to avert a confrontation between Brian Lara and a number of the Australian fieldsmen. I have mentioned this event in much greater detail in the West Indies chapter. To their credit, the captains ensured that was the end of it and we were treated to Taylor and Walsh shaking hands on the field, sort of like a world title prize fight! I hope it never happens again.

Umpires are often blamed for a player going over the edge. This is usually when we get a decision horribly wrong. When we do, it can very rarely be rectified so it's a case of forget it and get on with the game much the same as when a fieldsman drops a batsmen on nought and he bats all day for a century. This is easy for an umpire to do providing he has the confidence not to be rattled. Less so for the player. He sees you as the reason for his possible demise from the team and therefore the possible loss of his livelihood and dreams.

I have spoken to team selectors from club to inter-national level and not one of them has been able to give me a definite instance where a player has been dropped because of an umpire's decision. A poor decision may well dent the confidence, but I would have to say that in my opinion players have not been dropped because of umpiring decisions.

Obviously when a team is not playing well they will look for reasons and excuses but to blame an umpire for one call or two gives them the chance to remove all responsibility for losing from their shoulders. Captains and coaches who permit a player to blame their failures on an umpire are doing an injustice to that particular player. These players must be told to put the disappointment behind them and prepare for the next time. Should the coaches and captains not go down this path, it fosters an improper outlook towards the ideals of the game itself.

Cricket is lucky in one aspect and that is where coaches are not permitted under the ICC Code of Conduct to publicly criticise umpires or indulge in conduct which might bring the game into disrepute. Other sports do not seem to be all that aware of the image they portray in letting coaches get away with such conduct. On one occasion a few years ago, Phil Gould, who was coach of the Sydney City Roosters rugby league team and a well regarded tactician came up with a novel way of making his point about referees.

In a match between his team and Manly at Brookvale Oval, Gould was so incensed when he felt his team was on the wrong side of the penalty count that he sent a message out to his captain to organise a 'walk off'. What a silly way to make a protest and to my mind it was an absolute disgrace. Trying to publicy humiliate a referee or official must be the lowest act that a coach can dream up. Who was he trying to protect? His team for infringing the rules and conceding penalties? Or was he just trying to deflect criticism away from the fact that his own players were not carrying out his game plan? There is an old saying that the coach cannot actually play on behalf of his team but Gould was doing the next best thing. I reckon a $100 000 fine should have been imposed.

Thankfully this type of attitude is not part of cricket even if some coaches would like it to be.

CHAPTER ELEVEN

LIGHTER MOMENTS

A player who is poetry in motion to watch is Mark Waugh. His reputation as a laid-back 'no worries' cricketer is somewhat misplaced and he gives the impression that things come so easily and naturally to him, that he doesn't care when he gets out. In fact I think he hurts just as much as anyone when he fails to score many runs. Mark has an interest in horse racing and has raced a couple of pacers with some success. He also enjoys his time away from the cricket field visiting racecourses during the long Australian season. I quite often run into him charging around the betting rings and one occasion last season typifies both our characters.

I arrived in Perth on the Saturday morning in preparation for umpiring the One Day International on Sunday. Being such a warm sunny day I decided the best relaxation for me would be to make my way out to Ascot Racecourse making use of my 'ex's'. The Australian team had arrived on the Thursday and went down the south coast to Mandurah to build up some team spirit, (it had been a lean summer so far) by catching crabs and enjoying time away from the hustle and bustle of city life.

On arrival at Ascot, the first person I saw was Mark Waugh, with the form guide sticking out of his back pocket and a wad of notes in his hand ready for a confrontation with the bookies.

'Aren't the crabs still biting?' I asked. Mark replied, 'Nah, you can only eat so many and anyway I was lonely down at the local TAB. Ricky Ponting is not playing and none of the team are keen on punting on the horses so I decided to come back to see some action.'

After a frantic afternoon trying to pull off a few plunges we caught a taxi back to the Hyatt. Although my losses were enough to curtail a follow up evening at the casino, somehow I still managed to end up paying for the taxi fare! I guess cricketers are still very careful with their money.

Mark's exploits on the track will never be as well documented as his cricketing deeds although sometimes his racing background is used as a way of trying to unsettle him. Earlier last season Mark had not scored too many runs in the Test series against New Zealand and the Kiwis were not about to let him forget it. When he came to the crease in the third Test in Perth, a few choice comments were made in an attempt to unsettle him. The one I liked was 'Come on, chaps, let's give him plenty of time to read the form guide.' Unfortunately it didn't work as Mark played himself back into form with plenty of runs including hitting Daniel Vettori onto the roof of the Lillee Marsh Stand. It remains the biggest hit ever at the WACA Ground.

I'll never forget my first Test in Adelaide. It was Australia v India and my partner was to be Peter McConnell. However, the name on everyone's lips was that of one Sachin Tendulkar then the teenage sensation of the Indian team. He was to be trapped plumb in front and I obliged with the LBW decision. When we were leaving the ground later that evening (much later) a punter stumbled out of the Chappelli bar and began to engage in what I though to be meaningless conversation. He had something to get off his chest however and was determined to tackle me about it.

'By the way, thanks for ruining my day, you've got me in big trouble,' when he eventually said something that I could understand.

'What do you mean,' I enquired rather hesitantly, trying to think what on earth I had done to a cause a complete stranger so much grief.

'Well, I told my wife I was going to watch Tendulkar bat and I would be home to mow the lawn as soon as he got out and you were silly enough to fire him out at 11.05 this morning.'

I guess he may not have been the only one wanting to see Tendulkar bat but it's good to know I had no effect on his career.

I was always a frustrated back rower in my rugby days. It was the best position for me though as it doesn't matter if you are late to the scrum—just stick your head down and rest. My junior team had a hot shot fullback with a massive kicking game so when he saw the forwards needed a rest he would reef the ball miles into touch. By the time the ball had been recovered we had almost caught our breath.

With such a distinguished rugby background I was delighted to be invited as a guest speaker for the New South Wales Rugby Union Referees Annual Dinner. It is always grand to be able to mingle with the referees and umpires from other sports and you never stop learning. I opened my talk by giving my views on All Black Richard Loe's tackle on Australian winger Paul Carroza who had just touched down for a try in the corner. Loe arrived late and gave Carroza a broken nose with a well aimed elbow. I explained that I thought the tackle was quite legal because Loe did not straighten his arm at any stage during delivery.

John McGruther, the President of the NSW Cricketers' Club brought me a drink one night just prior to me leaving to

umpire in the West Indies. I had been appointed to do two Tests and they were following the abandoned match at Sabina Park, Jamaica. My matches were to be in Trinidad and Guyana. John usually travels on supporters tours with the Australian team through the Caribbean and he relayed a story he had heard about umpires in the West Indies.

A West Indian umpire died and was greeted at the Pearly Gates by St Peter.

'What honest deed have you accomplished on earth that would entitle you to residence in Heaven,' asked St Peter.

'Well, St Peter, I was a cricket umpire and to prove my honesty and integrity to the people of the world, I gave Brian Lara out leg before wicket during a Test match in Trinidad,' replied the umpire.

St Peter was very impressed: 'That was very noble of you and certainly proves you are welcome here, please come on in. By the way, who won the Test,' he added.

'No-one yet, I gave Lara out yesterday and today is only day two,' said the umpire.

CHAPTER TWELVE

THE BOWLERS

So far in this book I have mentioned some excellent batting performances and picked a world team with my reasons for selecting these players. One of the things that is largely forgotten in cricket is the part played by the workhorse of the game—the bowler. Batsmen score exciting centuries or bat for hours displaying powers of concentration that make them such special players. They receive accolades by fans who witness their feats and superlatives are written in newspapers and books about their grace and style.

The fact that it is a team game probably takes away some of the glory that bowlers should be accorded. Batsmen may say 'We scored the runs to give the bowlers a chance'. It can develop into a merry-go-round about who is the most important team member but my previous membership of the fast bowlers club 'Fastus Thickious' means I can only give argument to support the bowlers.

An umpire has to control the game according to the laws with absolute fairness and impartiality but what cricket watcher (myself included) cannot feel sympathy for the poor old fast bowler. He has slaved away all day on an unresponsive pitch, usually termed 'a highway' in stifling heat and he sees a simple regulation catch put down by one of his fielders. The batsman capitalises on his luck by slamming the very next ball straight back over the bowler's head for four runs. It is inevitably the last ball of the over and the umpire is given the task of handing the distraught bowler his cap. This is not the time to make small talk and it is best to allow him to let off steam with a few profanities and the umpire can beat a hasty retreat to square leg and out of the line of fire.

I have always taken the view that bowlers are the players that umpires need to have a special rapport with. We are dealing with the bowler every ball of the match and it can make for a long and difficult afternoon if the relationship gets a little touchy. We hold their caps and sweaters, judge no balls and answer their appeals on a ball to ball basis and my view has always been that I want a hassle free day. Sure we are going to have differing opinions on decisions but my preference is for working with rather than against members of my old fraternity.

I remember my first Sheffield Shield match when Mike Whitney handed me his cap and said 'left arm over'. Luckily for me I have had the greatest bowlers in the world do the same and I regard it as a special privilege to hold their gear and watch them go about their work. Fast bowling especially is a thankless task and the fitness and dedication that modern day bowlers exhibit is often overlooked. They struggle through with sore backs and blisters but by and large they enjoy their work and I for one will always appreciate a special performance and I have been witness to quite a few.

Bowlers such as Shane Warne, Alan Donald, Glenn McGrath, Mushtaq Ahmed, Wasim Akram, Craig McDermott, Merv Hughes, Greg Matthews, Curtly Ambrose, Courtney Walsh have, all at times, put up magnificent performances. I feel that the best individual bowling performance however was not by any of these bowlers and it came from a man that I could not find a place for in my world team, one Angus Fraser of England. When I arrived in Barbados in April 1994, England had already lost the series. They were three nil down and had just come off a frightful hiding in Trinidad being bowled out for 49 with Ambrose taking seven wickets.

The Kensington Oval, Barbados is generally accepted as being a batsman's paradise and bowlers were not expected to take the headlines. This view would be strengthened after Alec Stewart had scored a century in the first innings. The thing is with cricket and especially umpiring, is to expect the unexpected, and Fraser did not let me or his team down. Gus completely routed the West Indies batting and finished with 8 for 76 in a performance that I would not have believed had I not seen it myself. In stifling heat on an unresponsive pitch Gus ripped the heart out of the batting to set up an unlikely win. All the dismissals were either bowled, LBW or caught in the slips cordon which is a fair indication of the impeccable line and length which Fraser kept.

There were some stages during his spell when he seemed to be struggling and I am sure he was. You just cannot bowl for such long periods in that type of heat without feeling exhausted. It was at these times that I wished I could have loaned Gus some of my oxygen. But with constant support from Mike Atherton and his team mates Fraser somehow managed to summon the strength to keep on charging in to bowl.

Alec Stewart scored another fine century in the second innings to complete a fantastic double for him but it was definitely Gus Fraser who was my man of the match. I am yet to see a greater performance with the ball even though Fraser was to take 12 wickets in a similar performance at Trinidad some four years later. The pitch on that occasion however was far more responsive to seam bowling than the one rolled out at Barbados.

Another great performance from a bowler, this time a spinner, came from Greg Matthews the New South Wales off-spinner. A Sheffield Shield match between New South Wales and Western Australia at the Sydney Cricket Ground looked likely to end in a draw when Western Australia started the final day with all ten wickets in hand. Greg finished with 8 for 52 and it had to be the ultimate performance in the art of spin bowling. Right from ball one Matthews had the ball on a string. The classic loop through the air, the drift towards first slip then the vicious turn back on pitching made for an impossible day for the Western Australians. It was not as if the batting was inferior either. How could it be with the likes of Damien Martyn, Justin Langer, Tom Moody and Geoff Marsh but on this day they had no answer to Matthews' guile.

Days such as this make it a pleasure to be a witness to remarkable performances which cricket seems to be produce just when the match seems destined for a draw. Many people have not been complimentary in their remarks about Greg Matthews and I admit he is a bit 'different'. With his cricketing ability and brain however he has the happy knack of being able to read a player's thoughts and is a master at building and maintaining pressure. This goes for pressuring umpires as well and you always know you will be exhausted at the end of the day. I know I always was and I am sure I must have woken up from a deep sleep some nights during a game answering one of Greg's trademark appeals. Not my worst nightmare but close to it!

Talking about bowlers would not be complete without mentioning Shane Warne. Any bowler who has taken over 300 Test wickets must be special but nothing compares with Shane Warne spinning out of the rough. He is the biggest turner of the ball I have ever seen and some people say he doesn't need the extra advantage of using rough areas caused by the bowler's follow through. It is one thing to have the area there but it takes a very special bowler to make proper use of it.

At the Sydney Cricket Ground in 1996 against the West Indies, Warne removed not only Jimmy Adams but the champion Brian Lara with deliveries that spun out of the rough and bowled both of them. Until those dismissals on the last day, the match looked like it would head for a draw. The West Indies team had played Warne fairly well and armed with their left-handers it seemed like they had got the better of the duel. The ball had been spinning but no more than usual and it had certainly not caused batsmen from either side any real dramas. Warne changed all that with those two deliveries and the rest of the batsmen capitulated fairly quickly.

It is of no surprise to me that Shane has developed shoulder problems. The amount of spin he imparts on the ball is enormous and with the leg spin action being quite unorthodox I have never been certain how long the body can keep doing this as well as he has done in the past.

My playing career started with me being able to bowl a decent outswinger and finished with the only swing on the ball being when it was hit high back over my head for six by some grateful batsmen. I wonder how many batsmen I kept in good form with my inocuous deliveries? Retirement was a good option and umpiring opened up a whole new world.

I now enjoy the battles in Test cricket between bat and ball even though everything seems to be stacked against the fast bowler these days and the exciting spin of Warne and Mushtaq enthrals both player and spectator alike. My greatest thrill though is watching a beautifully delivered outswinger take the edge of the bat and fly through to the slips or wicket keeper. To me that is pure heaven.

CHAPTER THIRTEEN

SO YOU WANT
TO BECOME
AN INTERNATIONAL
UMPIRE?

Umpires do not just appear in the middle of the Sydney Cricket Ground or Lords—there is a lot of work to be done and training and experience to be gained before we are allowed to grace these grounds. Not many people are aware or even care about the steps that umpires must take before we put our selves under scrutiny.

Different countries have varying methods of recruiting umpires. England for example only recruit former first class players for their county cricket panel. There have been a couple of exceptions and Nigel Plews is one who did not play at that level but by and large the requirement is to have played at first class level. This system is defended by the England and Wales Cricket Board as providing umpires who will get more respect from the players but I am yet to be convinced it really produces the best umpires. I back this up by saying that most other umpires on the ICC International Panel have not played to first class level and they are every bit as competent as the English umpires.

I know from my own experiences that umpiring cannot be learnt in a week and merely obtaining a certificate on passing an examination of the laws is only the beginning. Our progression to the top ranks is similar in many ways to that of the players and the first step is to umpire in district or club cricket. I started out doing fourth grade in the Sydney Cricket Association and progressed to second grade and then first grade. This took me three years. I was then given control of some New South Wales Colts and Second Eleven matches before finally getting my initial Sheffield Shield appointment in February 1989.

It took me four years to reach this level and I thought I had learnt enough to be prepared for Test cricket. I still had some more learning to do though and the eight Sheffield Shield games prior to my first Test match provided me with much more experience and confidence.

The help I was given along the way by the New South Wales Cricket Umpires' Association was invaluable. They have a wonderful structure of training classes and the knowledge from within the Association just cannot be bought. I was lucky to have expert help from Tom Brooks, Ted Wykes and Dick French all former Test match umpires. In their own way they imparted knowledge which I was able to use to build my career and I will forever be grateful for having such great men from which I could learn the tricks of the trade.

Not enough experience though as I finally realised when I walked out on to the Adelaide Oval with Peter McConnell in January 1992. The step up from club cricket to Sheffield

Shield is quite large but nowhere near as huge as the Sheffield Shield to Test cricket leap.

I must profess to a continuing 'on the job' learning process but I suppose this is the same with players—the selectors never really can be sure if a player has the ability to step up and be successful. It is after all, the ultimate level and umpire selectors do not necessarily have a crystal ball either.

Much has been said and written about the talent identification and fast tracking of umpires to international level. I am not really sure if I agree with the idea as all umpires will admit to being in unknown territory when they attain each extra level of success. Should former first class players begin to show an interest in becoming umpires I agree that fast tracking would be appropriate in those cases as they are fully aware of the pressures on cricketers and umpires. Up until now however, players retiring from first class cricket, have shown no interest whatsoever in taking up umpiring so we shall have to wait some time yet to see if such a fast tracking system would work.

Once attaining Test match level in Australia the world is your oyster as the saying goes. Each year the nine Test-playing nations nominate two umpires to represent them on the National Grid Panel of Umpires which is operated by the International Cricket Council in London. England, who have fully professional umpires, nominate four umpires making a total panel of twenty. These umpires are then used for Test matches abroad as well as various one day international tournaments such as Sharjah. With the amount of cricket played these days and providing your own form stands up, there is the possibility of umpiring about three Test matches overseas each year. I have done eleven such Tests since April 1994 as well as a tournament in Sharjah and the Commonwealth Games in Malaysia.

So the rewards are there for all umpires who have the aspirations to become an international umpire but be prepared for a rocky ride along the way. The press can be overbearing yet kind, the television coverage can be cruel but gratifying and the players can be downright arrogant and dismissive. We have to accept though that we are not there to be the stars of the show as that position quite rightly belongs with the players.

Whichever way you see or treat the game of cricket, I can only say that the rewards have far outweighed the negatives during my career in this great game called cricket.

UMPIRING STATISTICS

TEST MATCHES

January 25–29, 1992	Australia	India	Adelaide
January 2–6, 1993	Australia	West Indies	Sydney
January 23–26, 1993	Australia	West Indies	Adelaide
November 12–16, 1993	Australia	New Zealand	Perth
November 26–29, 1993	Australia	New Zealand	Hobart
December 3–7, 1993	Australia	New Zealand	Brisbane (TV)
December 26–30, 1993	Australia	South Africa	Melbourne
January 29–February 1, 1994	Australia	South Africa	Adelaide
April 8–13, 1994	West Indies	England	Bridgetown
April 16–21, 1994	West Indies	England	St John's
January 1–5 1995	Australia	England	Sydney
March 4–8, 1995	New Zealand	South Africa	Auckland
November 17–20, 1995	Australia	Pakistan	Hobart
November 30, December 4, 1995	South Africa	England	Johannesburg
December 26–30, 1995	Australia	Sri Lanka	Melbourne
June 6–9, 1996	England	India	Edgbaston
June 20–24, 1996	England	India	Lords
November 29–December 3, 1996	Australia	West Indies	Sydney
January 2–6, 1997	South Africa	India	Cape Town
February 1–3, 1997	Australia	West Indies	Perth
February 14–18, 1997	New Zealand	England	Christchurch
November 20–23, 1997	Australia	New Zealand	Perth
January 2–5, 1998	Australia	South Africa	Sydney
February 13–17, 1998	West Indies	England	Port of Spain
February 27–March 2, 1998	West Indies	England	Georgetown
June 18–22, 1998	England	South Africa	Lords

ONE DAY INTERNATIONALS

December 14, 1991	West Indies	India	Adelaide
January 11, 1992	West Indies	India	Brisbane
January 14, 1992	Australia	India	Sydney
December 8, 1992	Australia	West Indies	Sydney
December 17, 1992	Pakistan	West Indies	Sydney
January 12, 1993	Australia	Pakistan	Melbourne
January 18, 1993	Australia	West Indies	Melbourne
December 14, 1993	Australia	South Africa	Sydney
January 9, 1994	Australia	South Africa	Brisbane
January 23, 1994	Australia	South Africa	Sydney
January 25, 1994	Australia	South Africa	Sydney
December 6, 1994	Australia	England	Sydney
December 15, 1994	Australia	Zimbabwe	Sydney
October 11, 1995	Sri Lanka	West Indies	Sharjah
October 13, 1995	Pakistan	West Indies	Sharjah
October 15 , 1995	Pakistan	West Indies	Sharjah
October 17, 1995	Pakistan	Sri Lanka	Sharjah
October 20, 1995	Sri Lanka	West Indies	Sharjah
December 21, 1995	Australia	Sri Lanka	Sydney
January 7, 1996	Australia	West Indies	Brisbane
January 12, 1996	Australia	Sri Lanka	Perth
January 16, 1996	Australia	Sri Lanka	Melbourne
January 18, 1996	Australia	Sri Lanka	Melbourne
December 8, 1996	Australia	West Indies	Sydney
January 12, 1997	Australia	West Indies	Perth
January 16, 1997	Australia	Pakistan	Melbourne
January 18, 1997	Pakistan	West Indies	Sydney
December 7, 1997	Australia	New Zealand	Adelaide
December 17, 1997	Australia	New Zealand	Melbourne
January 18, 1998	Australia	South Africa	Perth
January 23, 1998	Australia	South Africa	Melbourne
January 26, 1998	Australia	South Africa	Sydney
January 27, 1998	Australia	South Africa	Sydney

OTHER LIMITED OVER MATCHES

January 12, 1995	Australia 'A'	England	Sydney
January 15, 1995	Australia	Australia 'A'	Sydney
January 17, 1995	Australia	Australia 'A'	Melbourne

SHEFFIELD SHIELD

February 22–25, 1989	NSW	Tasmania	Sydney
December 15–18, 1989	NSW	Victoria	Sydney
January 6–9, 1990	NSW	W.A.	Sydney
February 15–18, 1990	NSW	S.A.	Sydney
March 9–12, 1990	NSW	Tasmania	Sydney
January 31–Feb 3, 1991	NSW	W.A.	Sydney
March 7–10, 1991	NSW	Queensland	Sydney
November 8–11, 1991	NSW	Victoria	Sydney
March 7–9, 1992	NSW	W.A.	Sydney
November 6–9, 1992	NSW	Victoria	Sydney
December 11–14, 1992	NSW	Queensland	Sydney
February 3–6, 1993	NSW	W.A.	Sydney
March 11–14, 1993	NSW	S.A.	Sydney
March 26–30, 1993	NSW	Queensland	Sydney
December 18–21, 1993	NSW	Victoria	Sydney
March 17–20, 1994	NSW	Queensland	Sydney
March 25–29, 1994	NSW	Tasmania	Sydney
November 18–21, 1994	NSW	Queensland	Sydney
December 9–12, 1994	NSW	Tasmania	Sydney
January 27–30, 1995	NSW	Victoria	Sydney
March 24–28, 1995	Queensland	S.A.	Brisbane
October 26–29, 1995	NSW	Tasmania	Sydney
November 2–5, 1995	Tasmania	Queensland	Hobart
February 13–16, 1996	Victoria	S.A.	Melbourne
March 23–26, 1996	Victoria	Queensland	Melbourne

March 30–April 3, 1996	S.A.	W.A.	Adelaide
November 6–9, 1996	Queensland	Tasmania	Brisbane
November 15–18, 1996	W.A.	Tasmania	Perth
March, 13–16, 1997	Queensland	S.A.	Brisbane
March 21–25, 1997	W.A.	Queensland	Perth
October 15–18, 1997	S.A.	Tasmania	Adelaide
October 31, November, 3, 1997	Tasmania	W.A.	Hobart
March 12–15, 1998	Victoria	Tasmania	Melbourne
March 20–23, 1998	W.A.	Tasmania	Perth

OTHER FIRST CLASS MATCHES

November 22–25, 1990	NSW	Wellington	North Sydney
January 13–16, 1991	NSW	England	Albury
November 14–17, 1992	Australian XI	West Indies	Hobart
November 20–23, 1993	NSW	West Indies	Sydney
October 29–November 1, 1993	NSW	New Zealand	Newcastle
November 12–15, 1994	NSW	England	Newcastle

AUSTRALIAN DOMESTIC LIMITED OVERS

October 16, 1990	NSW	Tasmania	Sydney
October 20, 1990	NSW	Victoria	Sydney
October 15, 1991	NSW	Victoria	North Sydney
October 20, 1991	NSW	Tasmania	North Sydney
January 31, 1993	NSW	Tasmania	Sydney
February 20, 1993	NSW	Victoria	Sydney
October 24, 1993	NSW	Tasmania	North Sydney
February 6, 1994	NSW	W.A.	Sydney
March 5, 1994	S.A.	W.A.	Adelaide
March 12, 1994	NSW	W.A.	Sydney
October 16, 1994	NSW	S.A.	North Sydney

February 25, 1995	W.A.	S.A.	Perth
February 4, 1996	NSW	S.A.	Sydney
February 25, 1996	NSW	W.A.	Sydney
March 3, 1996	Queensland	W.A.	Brisbane
October 13, 1996	NSW	W.A.	North Sydney
February 23, 1997	W.A.	Victoria	Perth
March 2, 1997	W.A.	Queensland	Perth
October 5, 1997	NSW	S.A.	North Sydney
February 8, 1998	NSW	Tasmania	Sydney

Summary of all Matches and Games Umpired

TESTS	25
ONE DAY INTERNATIONAL	33
SHEFFIELD SHIELD	34
OTHER FIRST CLASS	6
STATE ONE DAY	20
COMMONWEALTH GAMES	4